Advance Reviews

Science's Dead End, Religions' Opening, and a Restart for Meaning surprised me in the best way possible. It was far more insightful than I anticipated, wrapped in a language that is both accessible and engaging. Christopher does an excellent job of weaving together extensive research and references from various works, which I found particularly compelling. This approach offers readers a gateway to explore a broader range of literature, sparking curiosity to delve deeper into those mentioned.

The book presents a tapestry of examples and cases where the divine or religious experience intersects with realms that science struggles to explain. While he doesn't inundate the reader with an overload of details, Christopher provides just the right amount of information to spark intrigue and understanding. This balance makes the book an easy yet thought-provoking read.

I would wholeheartedly recommend this book to anyone eager to explore the nuanced relationship between science and the divine. It's a thoughtful journey through the mysteries of our world, encouraging us to consider how the divine weaves into the fabric of everyday life.

◆ ◆ ◆

I recommend this book as it presents a broadened view of forces which acts on an individual life. It also argues that science has a long way to go in presenting a convincing argument for a purely material universe.

After decades of time and billions of dollars of DNA decoding and brain research and mapping, traditional scientific methods have resulted in a surprisingly disappointing lack of practical knowledge useful to our lives and health. This is the premise of Ted Christopher's new book *Science's Dead End, Religion's Opening, and a Restart for Meaning*.

Those without at least a basic understanding of philosophy and physics might find this work a bit difficult to fully digest. To aid the reader, Christopher includes several thought-provoking stories, facts, and copious references. His conclusion is that there is more to being human than is encoded in our DNA and stored in our brains (the materialistic view) and for some reason many scientists refuse to even consider any other possibilities.

◆ ◆ ◆

The thesis of this book is very relevant as it drives home the question about the ultimate meaning of human life. It is important to realize that pure analytical science cannot answer all the questions, and that humans are more than biological, physical, and neurological systems.

Science's Dead End, Religions' Opening, and a Restart for Meaning

By
Ted Christopher

Copyright © 2024 by Ted Christopher
All rights reserved.

ISBN: 978-1629672809
Library of Congress Control Number: Pending

All rights reserved. No part of this book may be reproduced in any form or by any electronic or mechanical means, including information storage and retrieval systems, without written permission from the author, except in the case of a reviewer, who may quote brief passages embodied in critical articles or in a review.

Trademarked names appear throughout this book. Rather than use a trademark symbol with every occurrence of a trademarked name, names are used in an editorial fashion, with no intention of infringement of the respective owner's trademark.

The information in this book is distributed on an "as is" basis, without warranty. Although every precaution has been taken in the preparation of this work, neither the author nor the publisher shall have any liability to any person or entity with respect to any loss or damage caused or alleged to be caused directly or indirectly by the information contained in this book.

Rev 24-1210

Dedicated to my refugee friends
and other sincere people
with heretical views.

Contents

- **PREFACE – AN OVERVIEW** 5
- **CHAPTER 1 - OBVIOUS CHALLENGES TO SCIENTIFIC MATERIALISM** 11
  - 1. Prodigies 11
  - 2. Terminal Lucidity 21
  - 3.a. Initial Taboo Phenomena 26
  - 3.b. More Taboo, Mostly from Elizabeth Mayer's Accounts 30
  - 3.c. Taboo Follow-up from Mark Gober's Upside Down Book 39
  - 4. Transgender Children 43
  - 5. Hyperthymesia 46
  - 6. Multiple Personality Disorder 48
  - 7. Personality Changes Following Heart Transplants 51
  - 8. Medium-based Potential Insights 59
  - 9. Our Innate Religious Perspective 69
  - 10. Discussions on Behavioral Challenges 72
- **CHAPTER 2 - SCIENCE'S BIG PROBLEM - THE MISSING HERITABILITY** 77
  - 1. Introduction 77
  - 2. "Dudes, get back to us if and when you have something to report" 93
  - 3. Some Additional Context and Possible Explanations 104
  - 4. Some Perspective from Physics and Psychiatry 115
  - 5. Considering Evolutionary Challenges 124
  - 5.a. - Primate Color Vision 126
  - 5.b. - Wasps versus Cockroaches and Other Instinctive Behaviors 127
- **CHAPTER 3 - AN INTRODUCTION TO RELIGIONS VIA EXPERIENCES OF SELF/EGO TRANSCENDENCE** 133
  - 1. Experiences of Unity or Transcendence 133
  - 2. *And There Was Light* 135
  - 3. Buddhism, Enlightenment, and Sam Harris' Waking Up 140
  - Some Conclusions About Meditation and Religious Inquiry 161
- **CHAPTER 4 - FINAL DISCUSSIONS** 171
- **ABOUT THE AUTHOR** 191
- **ACKNOWLEDGMENTS** 193
- **REFERENCES** 195

Preface – An Overview

The most influential contribution of modern science is its vision of life, which simply consists of DNA-driven molecular ensembles. A relatively concrete translation of this vision was presented by the biologist Ursula Goodenough:

> [a]ll of us, and scientists are no exception, are vulnerable to the existential shudder that leaves us wishing that the foundations of life were something other than just so much biochemistry and biophysics. The shudder, for me at least, is different from the encounters with nihilism that have beset my contemplation of the universe. There I can steep myself in cosmic Mystery. But the workings of life are not mysterious at all. They are obvious, explainable, and thermodynamically inevitable. And relentlessly mechanical. And bluntly deterministic. My body is some 10 trillion cells. Period. My thoughts are a lot of electricity flowing along a lot of membrane. My emotions are the result of neurotransmitters squirting on my brain cells. I look in the mirror and see the mortality and I find myself fearful, yearning for less knowledge, yearning to believe that I have a soul that will go to heaven and soar with the angels [Goodenough, pp.46-7].

That is the upshot of the contemporary molecular-only or bio-robotic vision of life. Of note here is that this nihilism is found in an arguably modern inspirational book, Goodenough's *The Sacred Depths of Nature*.

Additional insight is offered in the novelist Julian Barnes' fine book, *Nothing to be frightened of* [Barnes]. Barnes 'perceptive and literate work addressed death and along with it quite a bit of life. A relevant quote:

> We discover, to our surprise, that as [Richard] Dawkins memorably puts it, we are "survival machines - robot vehicles blindly programmed to preserve the selfish molecules known as genes". The paradox is that individualism - the triumph of free-thinking artists and scientists - has led us to a state of self-awareness in which we can now view ourselves as units of genetic obedience. My adolescent notion of self-construction - that vaguely, Englishly, existentialist ego-hope of autonomy - could not have been further from the truth. I thought the burdensome process of growing up ended with a man standing by himself at last - *homo erectus* at full height, *sapiens* in full wisdom - a fellow now cracking the whip on his own full account. This image ... must be replaced by the sense that, far from having a whip to crack, I am the very tip of the whip itself, and that what is cracking me is a long and inevitable plait of genetic material which cannot be shrugged or fought off. My 'individuality' may still be felt, and genetically provable; but it may be the very opposite of the achievement I once took it for [Barnes, pp.93-4].

Barnes's work is impressive in that he didn't romanticize science or appear to indulge in intellectual arrogance (although he might have indulged a bit in stylish writing). Overall, he comes across like a sincere person who takes life and truth seriously. What is notable, though, is that Barnes at no point in his book questioned science's material-only understanding of life (or materialism). I suggest from my own experience that this is consistent with contemporary intellectuals, certainly academics, and beyond this effectively many others.

For some additional context, the book opened with, "I don't believe in God, but I miss Him" [Barnes, p.3]. And somewhat to his credit, Barnes did take some shots at atheists, philosophers (his brother is one), and more generally modern lifestyles. But consistent with science, Barnes wrote" [n]ow, alone, we must consider what our Godless wonder might be for" [p.93] and Christianity is a "beautiful lie" [p.53]. He also suggested that modern alternative pursuits - the "secular modern heaven of self-fulfillment" - and their purported realization of happiness is "our chosen myth" [p.59].

Continuing with this modern intellectual onslaught, the psychologist and author Steven Pinker wrote with complete confidence:

> [i]n making sense of the world, there should be few occasions in which we are forced to concede "It just is" or "It's magic" or "Because I said so". The commitment to intelligibility is not a matter of brute faith, but gradually validates itself as more and more of the world becomes explicable in scientific terms. The processes of life, for example, used to be attributed to a mysterious elan vital; now we know they are powered by chemical and physical reactions among complex molecules [Pinker 2013].

Further, the presumed director of those molecules is of course the big molecule, DNA. Thus, Pinker later added that science's "understanding consists not in a mere listing of facts, but in deep and elegant principles, like the insight that life depends on a molecule that carries information, directs metabolism, and replicates itself" [Pinker 2013].

A basic point in this book is that Pinker's confident presentation was both a given and also obviously wrong. It is a given because for science - again with many in tow - it simply has to be true, if only to stay consistent with the views of physics and the imagined brilliance therein. It is wrong because it is trivial to find accepted/irrefutable behavioral phenomena that are extremely unlikely to be consistent with materialism and evolution. Thus this book will present a number of stunning behaviors as well as touch on the associated scientific divorce from acknowledging them. More generally and significantly, the book will also consider the extraordinary failures that have unfolded during the last 20 years of genomic searches. If life really "depends on a molecule that carries information, directs metabolism, and replicates itself" then why has 20 years of extensive, expensive, and presumed to be straightforward DNA (or genomic) searches - yielded an "absolutely beyond belief" "almost nothing" in terms of confirmed DNA origins? DNA maybe the unquestioned language of life for science, but it certainly isn't in reality.

If you happen to have some older genetic literature around you might list out some of the stated expectations with regard to the presumed genetic influences for disease susceptibilities and behavioral tendencies. These are connected with the fields of personal genomics and behavioral genetics, respectively. Then you might carefully check on the confirmed genomic (DNA) search findings. Conveniently, the confirmed findings make this a bit of a back-of-the-envelope exercise. Are there some preexisting DNA connections (and somewhat analogously some neural correlations) - yes, but the broad picture genetically (and also neurally) is very different. The generous extrapolations by science of limited materialist connections or correlations, paired with its determined denial of contrary evidence, has very likely set science up for a big fall.

This book will directly and tersely take on the scientific vision of life, as well as a bit of the associated hubris-heavy packaging. Of note is that while the numbers of overtly science-worshipping people maybe relatively small, the number of those - even among religious/alternative types - who accept the basic molecular-only package whilst perhaps wedging in some type of God factor or some form of quantum speculation-based magic, is very significant. If you want to make deeper sense of life then you had better face the stark implications of science's vision head-on.

Period. It should be a big embarrassment that in our time, presumed brilliant people studying unimaginably remote and irrelevant topics - like black holes - are taken as bearers of profundity.

About a year ago I started to put together a book covering a number of science-questioning topics as well as the associated potential support for religious beliefs including reincarnation. These topics I had been writing about mostly in the form of papers. A publisher, Scientific Research Publishing, contacted me with an interest in publishing it. I went ahead with their offer and they were quite helpful in getting *Meaning Beyond Molecules and Hubris* ready [Christopher 2023]. Unfortunately, they treated it in sort of an academic fashion. This book on the other hand is considerably shorter, more focused, and less expensive. Working as an outsider questioning science I found that trying to draw interest from academics is probably akin to selling Slurpees during the winter in Siberia.

For brevity I have limited this book to four chapters. The first chapter tours through 9 basic behavioral challenges to the scientific vision. The next chapter then discusses the unfolding genetics impasse, or the missing heritability problem. The third chapter then carefully looks at religious/mystical breakthrough experiences. If religious/mystical(/alternative) traditions are onto something general and meaningful (as thus perhaps reflected in the fact that we are born with religious/dualistic beliefs), then there should likely be psychological experiences consistent with that. Such phenomenon - unlike other aspects of religions - should be observable. Finally, the last chapter attempts to tie together the earlier material and discuss further the situation.

An implied message associated with science's vision of life is that frankly you would have to be stupid to question it. A basic message suggested herein is that collectively many of us moderners have been dimwits in uncritically accepting it.

Chapter 1 - Obvious Challenges to Scientific Materialism

1. Prodigies

One of the simplest ways to question the scientific vision is by looking at prodigal behaviors. There you can encounter some truly incredible abilities and inclinations. The plausibility of such phenomena, including an underlying DNA origin and evolutionary basis, is a good place to appreciate mental life's complexity and science's misplaced certainty. Of particular note here is that one of DNA's presumed roles is to provide "[t]he entire behavioral information available to the newborn" [Mayr, p.253].

A little further context here is that our species during its evolutionary trek branched off from chimpanzees. In so doing we left behind a life largely in trees, and moved on to spread out across Africa and then elsewhere. This complicated journey involved numerous interactions including those with other non-surviving hominids. But in general what type of scenario provided the relevant backdrop to the evolutionary specialization of our psyches (and of course our large brains)? Steven Pinker offered a straightforward answer:

> [o]ur minds are adopted to the small foraging bans in which our family spent ninety-nine percent of its existence, not the topsy-turvy contingencies we created since the agricultural and industrial revolutions [Pinker 1997, p.20].

Pinker additionally characterized the accompanying environmental or natural selection pressure as "a camping trip that never end[ed]" [Pinker 1997, p.207]. Sounds reasonable. Thus in a gross sense the demands encountered during primitive camping were then likely to have driven the development of our particular mental capabilities. Such a presumed development was naturally supposed to have a physical underpinning found in our natural selection-shaped DNA blueprints. Thus the historical changes in our mental capacities were supposed to reflect underlying changes to our DNA blueprints. The jump from this type of framework, though, to providing plausible explanations for prodigious mental capabilities is very difficult to imagine.

Getting a start here is a description of a musical prodigy as given in Darold A. Treffert's fine *Islands of Genius*:

> By age five Jay had composed five symphonies. His fifth symphony, which was 190 pages and 1328 bars in length was professionally recorded by the London Symphony Orchestra for Sony Records. On a *60 Minutes* program in 2006 Jay's parents stated that Jay began to draw little cellos on paper at age two. Neither parent was particularly musically inclined, and there were never any musical instruments, including a cello, in the home. At age three Jay asked if he could have a cello of his own. The parents took him to a music store and to their astonishment Jay picked up a miniature cello and began to play it. He had never seen a real cello before that day. After that he began to draw miniature cellos and placed them on music lines. That was the beginning of his composing.
>
> Jay says that the music just streams into his head at lightning speed, sometimes several symphonies running simultaneously. "My unconscious directs

my conscious mind at a mile a minute," he told the correspondent [Treffert, pp.55-6].

Treffert's book contains other examples that supported his conclusion that prodigal behavior typically involves "know[ing] things [that were] never learned" [Treffert, p.59].

Now switching consideration to another musical prodigy as described in Andrew Solomon's epic *Far From the Tree* [Solomon 2012]. Solomon began his chapter on prodigies with an account of Russian classical pianist Evgeny Kissin [Solomon 2012, pp.408-9]. Evgeny's mother and father were respectively a piano teacher and an engineer, and moreover they were living what Solomon characterized as Soviet Jewish Intelligentsia in Moscow. The parents had initially thought that Evgeny's sister, Alla, would follow her mother and play the piano, while Evgeny (or Zhenya) would follow his father and go an engineering route. At eleven months of age, though, the Evgeny managed to sing an entire Bach fugue after hearing his sister Alla practice it. Thereafter Evgeny reportedly pursued singing in response to just about "everything he heard". This became so relentless that his mother became quite concerned over it.

Then at twenty-six months Evgeny made an appearance at the piano. Evgeny:

> sat down at the piano and with one finger picked out some of the tunes he had been singing. The next day he did the same, and on the third day he played with both hands, using all of his fingers. He would listen to LPs and immediately play back the music. "Chopin's ballades, he would play with those little hands, and Beethoven sonatas, Liszt's rhapsodies," [his mom reported]. At three, he began improvising. He especially liked to make musical portraits of people.

He subsequently liked to quiz his family on these portraits.

Kissin displayed such exceptional skills that eventually led his reluctant mother to take him to a prominent piano teacher at Moscow's famous Gnessin State Musical College. As a result that teacher, Anna Pavlovna Kantor, would later report on the 5 year old Evgeny Kissin:

> I saw a light in him. Without knowing how to read music or the name of notes, he played everything. I asked him to translate a story into music. I said we were coming into a dark forest, full of wild animals, very scary, and then step by step the sun rises, and the birds start singing. He began in the piano's lower register, in a dark and dangerous place, and then, lighter and lighter, the birds awakening, the first rays of the sun, and finally a delightful, almost ecstatic melody, his hands running along the keys. I didn't want to teach him. Such imagination can be very fragile.

By age 7 he started to write down his compositions. Evgeny would later state that, "[w]hen I would return from school, I would, without taking my coat off, go to the piano and play". He then added, "I made my mother understand that that this was just what I needed".

Evgeny's development was remarkable and certainly would seem to have had a large innate component. Is it realistic to think that DNA could have been behind young Evgeny's musical inclination and aptitude?

Another notable prodigy was the historical musical savant Thomas Bethune or Blind Tom, considered here as described in Darold Treffert's remarkable Islands of Genius [Treffert, pp.87-92]. Blind Tom was born in 1849 as the son of the slaves, Charity and Domingo Wiggins. He and his parents were sold the following year to General James N. Bethune in Columbus, Georgia. General Bethune then allowed the blind infant Tom to have the run of his plantation. Although, Tom apparently had significant challenges in addition to his blindness - "[h]e was restless, explosive, and required constant supervision", he displayed a remarkable connection with music and more generally sound. This became readily apparent after his exposure to the piano playing of General Bethune's daughter. As Darold Treffert noted via a quote from a contemporary of Tom's, Dr. Edward Sequin:

> Till 5 or 6 years old he could not speak, scarce walk, and gave no other signs of intelligence than his everlasting thirst for music, but at 4 years already, if taken out of the corner where he laid dejected, and seated at the piano, he would play beautiful tunes; his little hands having already taken possession of the keys, and his wonderful ear of any combination of notes they had once heard.

Blind Tom somehow from a young age could simply hear some music and then play it back. Additionally, he could then store it up for future usage. His ultimate musical repertoire was estimated at about 7,000 pieces. He also demonstrated an analogous capacity to hear and then accurately repeat back verbiage he was exposed to, despite having a personal vocabulary which may have peaked in the vicinity of 100 words.

Starting at age 8 Blind Tom became a touring sensation and as such made a lot of money for the Bethunes. In conjunction with his very impressive performances there were those who tried to disprove or debunk his musical genius (along with his immense memory). Thus, as part of his performance routine there developed an opportunity for audience members to test Tom. In one such scenario during a White House performance, the 11 year old Tom faced some skeptical musicians who played two new compositions. One was about 13 pages in length and the other about 20 pages. Tom reportedly then played these two pieces back accurately. Reportedly, tests like these did little to reduce Tom's reputation.

Darold Treffert included a general assessment of Tom's musical prowess as provided by a panel of 16 expert musicians. The assessment included:

> [w]hether in his improvisations of performances of compositions by Gottschalk, Verdi, and others, in fact in every form of musical examination - and the experiments are too numerous to mention - he showed a capacity ranking him among the most wonderful phenomena in musical history.

Somehow Blind Tom, although reportedly difficult to train, found a way to be a phenomenal musician. This despite having a career that was significantly limited to a role as a commercial vehicle for his guardians. The author Mark Twain attended a number of Tom's concerts and admiringly referred to him as the "archangel".

As a sample of Tom's amazing abilities, in one of his regular acts he would simultaneously sing "Early in the Morning"; play "Fisher's Hornpipe" in C with his left hand; and play "Yankee Doodle" in B flat with his right hand. Additionally, Treffert noted some similarities between Tom's abilities and those of the modern musical savant, Leslie Lemke [Treffert, pp.93-109]. A note here on possible follow-up is that associated with both Blind Tom and Leslie Lemke there are a number of dedicated internet sites.

Another interesting contemporary prodigy story is that of the pianist Drew Petersen [Solomon 2012, pp.417-9]. Although, seemingly raised in a musically-modest family, Drew became an exceptional performer. As an infant Drew did not speak until his was three and a half years old, although he was clearly intelligent. In fact at 18 months he managed to point to a word that his mother had skipped while reading to him. Like other musical prodigies he exhibited a remarkable sensitivity to sound.

After some informal training with his mother, Drew then went on to start formal lessons at age five. He then skipped about six months of material and ended up within a year "performing Beethoven sonatas at the recital hall at Carnegie Hall and was flown to Italy to perform in a youth festival where the other youths were a decade older". Eventually, Drew's parents tried to get him to have lessons with a notable teacher at the Manhattan School of Music, Miyoko Lotto. Lotto, though, was initially hesitant. But after hearing him she later reported:

> [h]e could barely reach the pedals, but he played with every adult nuance you'd ever want. I thought, 'Oh my God, this really is genius. He's not mimicking and not being spoon-fed. His musicality comes from within'.

On the way to kindergarten one day Drew asked his mother, "[c]an I just stay home so I can learn something"? His mom later reflected, "[h]e was reading textbooks this big, and they're in class holding up a blowup M". Additionally, Drew, as is common with prodigies, demonstrated enormous self-determination. In Drew's case, his parents seemed to wisely brace against the hype associated with prodigies. As Solomon pointed out, "[t]hey never expected the life into which Drew has led them, but they were neither intimidated by it nor brash in pursuing it; it remained both a diligence and an art". In a relevant contrast, Solomon quoted Harvard professor of music, Robert Levin, on the lack of improvement associated with the contemporary trend of ambitious parents pushing their young piano-playing offspring towards demanding musical pieces.

In somewhat of a parallel, Drew's academic instincts and gifts had him halfway through a Harvard University degree at age 16 when he met Solomon. Drew then related to Solomon that he had thought he might find a topic at Harvard that equaled or even exceeded his interest in music. But Drew pointed out that that didn't happen and "I'm not sure I really want to". He also added, "I want a life in music".

Genetics should offer explanations for some of these prodigious phenomena. In Steven Pinker's *How the Mind Works* after a somewhat dismissive discussion about the overlapping phenomena of geniuses - as in they are pretty much like the rest of us - Pinker went on to add that they may "have been dealt a genetic hand of four aces" [Pinker 1997, pp.361-2]. From a scientific perspective, though, doesn't any explanation for exceptional intellects have to largely begin with DNA specifics? Scientifically what else could provide for the exceptional smarts and also inclinations? In his loose book, *From Bacteria to Bach and Back*, the philosopher Daniel C. Dennett claimed that (in italics), *"genes don't account for genius"* [Dennett, p.24]. A DNA basis for high intelligence might not fully explain productive geniuses since there have been plenty of high intelligence individuals who didn't produce noteworthy high-level works or breakthroughs. Nevertheless, the overlap between high intelligence and (productive) genius appears to dictate that such geniuses should have generous DNA contributions to their IQs. Furthermore, prodigies also tend to display strong innate drives which would appear to demand additional DNA support. With genetic contributions increasingly in question (as discussed in the next chapter) this adds to the mystery of prodigies and geniuses. It is truly astounding that some young children appear to hit the proverbial pavement running in a largely adult-focused fashion.

Darold Treffert whose longtime research focus has been on autism and savants concluded that:

> I must say, though, from my observations of prodigious savants and prodigies, it appears to me that it is the actual knowledge itself within an area of special expertise that is inherited [Treffert, p.91].

And along with that knowledge one might argue that in some cases a focused determination seems to be inherited too.

One final prodigy considered here is Kit Armstrong [Solomon 2012, p.456-7]. Kit's prodigious abilities showed up early. He was able to count at 15 months. His mother May taught him addition and subtraction at age two. He then went on to teach himself multiplication and division. Solomon suggests that at age three Kit was asking about things for which the theory of relativity was required for an explanation (though, this claim is of course extraordinary and probably tricky to establish). Kit's mother was not pushy in raising him. In fact she was concerned about his hyper-development pace and hoped he might "grow down" in kindergarten.

While completing second grade Kit also managed to finish off high school math. By age nine Kit was ready to try college and enrolled at Utah State University. At ten he toured Los Alamos National Laboratory with his music manager, Charles Hamlen. At Los Alamos a physicist took Hamlen aside and told him:

> unlike the postdoctoral physicists who usually visited, Kit was so bright that no one could 'find the bottom of this boy's knowledge'.

Within a few years Kit had a residency at MIT and there he helped edit some papers in chemistry, physics, and math. About Kit's apparent ability to pick up so much information and expertise his mother said:

> [h]e just understands all things. Someday, I want to work with parents of disabled children, because I know their bewilderment is like mine. I had no idea how to be a mother to Kit, and there was no place to find out.

If scientists would consider children like Kit they might share in that bewilderment.

Kit Armstrong's lasting extraordinary contributions, though, have been with his piano performances and composing. When Kit was five years old his mother May wanted to find him a hobby and she went outside of her own interests and decided to try piano lessons. Consistent with his general intellectual prowess Kit raced ahead on the piano. After his first lesson Kit returned home to make his own staff paper and then proceeded to attempt a composition. Solomon reports that Kit's facility with the language of music had "come to him whole" and that he could simply hear music on the radio and then "play it back".

To further connect Kit to music his mom moved them to London so he could study at the Royal Academy of Music. There he became the first student of the expert pianist Alfred Brendel, someone who coincidentally also did not come from a musical background. When Kit was thirteen a journalist who was a strong critic of placing children in serious performance situations attended one of his concerts. After that performance the journalist wrote:

> [h]is playing was so cultured, his joy in performing so obvious, his commitment as he stretched his small frame to reach the low notes so total, that my objections seemed mean-spirited.

You can also read about Kit Armstrong's career on the internet.

One interesting phenomenon appears among some of these prodigy examples. That is that some of these super-bright kids would seem to have had a choice between moving ahead rapidly in academic or in musical careers. At least amongst this admittedly small sample of prodigies they went with music. One might then wonder if there are other individuals who could have been exceptional at music but instead chose an academic focus. I wonder if there is a tendency to go with the music route then that could reflect something basic. Perhaps music tends to be more fun than straight intellectual work.

The realm of prodigies is home to some phenomenal and clearly science-challenging behaviors. Could evolution have established a collection of DNA ingredients that account for prodigies and thus provide some support for Pinker's general assertion about science's "[m]aking sense of the world"?

2. Terminal Lucidity

Terminal lucidity is a phenomenon in which people inexplicably return to mental coherence shortly before death after appearing to be lost to "dull, unconscious, or mentally ill" conditions, sometimes for years. The physical/neural plausibility of such rejuvenations is hard to fathom.

A general introduction of terminal lucidity is found in a *Scientific American* blog piece by the psychologist Jesse Bering, "One Last Goodbye/ The Strange Case of Terminal Lucidity" [Bering]. Bering considered something that was perhaps first described in the modern era in an article by German biologist Michael Nahm [Nahm 2009]. Nahm described terminal lucidity as:

> The (re-)emergence of normal or unusually enhanced mental abilities in dull, unconscious, or mentally ill patients shortly before death, including considerable elevation of mood and spiritual affectation, or the ability to speak in a previously unusual spiritualized and elated manner [Nahm 2009].

In a subsequent article, Nahm along with Bruce Greyson, mentioned that in a study of 49 cases, 41 of them involved surprising verbalizations during the last week of life [Nahm and Greyson 2009]. In 21 of the cases the verbalizations came on the same day as death. In some cases severely mentally impaired individuals had gradually returned to close to normal lucidity before their death. This included mention of a case involving a man who had been catatonic for nearly 2 decades before his reemergence to a near normal state.

Additional cases have shown up elsewhere including in articles in *The Guardian* [Godfrey] and in *Psychology Today* [Mendoza]. As one doctor pointed out after reviewing surveys, "it is safe to say that this phenomena exists, and likely exists more often than we expect" [Godfrey]. In such articles some poignant episodes recalled by relatives who witnessed miraculous rejuvenations of seemingly cognitively-lost individual were given. In one such case a witness recalled her grandmother rejuvenation:

> She was sitting up in bed, smiling as we walked in. For the next two hours she laughed and joked, completely cognitive, coherent ... lucid. A lifetime of memory had returned, and we took advantage of it as she regaled with episodes from her past. My mum [mother], who knew many of them, quietly verified them. Her funny, eloquent, vibrant mother had returned. 'It all came back to her in one rush,' remembers my mum. 'It was like a bolt of lightning. The clouds cleared.' After we left that afternoon, my grandma slipped back into a semi-conscious state, soon not knowing who my mother was, and died within days [Godfrey].

The most striking case involved a severely disabled young woman named Anna ("Kathe") Katherina Ehmer [Nahm and Grayson 2013; Bering]. Her episode occurred in 1922 and apparently had substantial verification as Kathe was a patient in a mental hospital and her sudden lucidity was observed by the hospital's chief physician Wilhem Wittneben and also its director Friedrich Happich. Kathe had been born with severe disabilities and as such had never spoken and moreover seemed detached from her environment. And yet in her last half-hour of life she somehow reportedly sung (in a spiritualized fashion) and this in particular involved the repeated phrase, "*Where does the soul find its home, its peace? Peace, peace, heavenly peace!*" In another article it was reported that those "present were rendered speechless themselves; some sobbed in bewilderment; others felt they had witnessed a miracle of the soul" [Burnett III].

Moving along now to an excellent clinical review found in the *Archives of Gerontology and Geriatrics*, "Terminal lucidity: A review and a case collection" [Nahm *et al* 2012]. In that paper's opening sentence it suggests that what is now referred to as "terminal [or paradoxical] lucidity", "has been reported over the past 250 years, but has received little attention". Given the striking nature of this phenomenon the lack of attention appears surprising. Perhaps, though, the authors' observation that "discussions and case reports" became "almost absent in the medical literature of the 20th century" reflects the overwhelming clout of materialism in the modern medical ranks.

Nahm *et al*'s review presentation includes details with regards to 19 clinical cases (excluding Anna Katrina Ehmer's). Herein I narrow the presentation down to 4 of those cases and moreover suggest that interested readers might consider obtaining the fine (4 and 1/2 page) article for themselves. I will minimize the traumatic nature of some of the patients' experiences.

The first case considered here occurred in 1822 and involved a 6 year old boy who had fallen on a nail which had thus penetrated his forehead. This was followed by subsequent "headaches and mental disturbances" and by age 17 "he was in constant pain, extremely melancholic, and starting to lose his memory". He also, "fantasized, blinked continuously, and looked for hours at particular objects". He was later admitted to a hospital after regularly vomiting and while a patient therein during the next 18 days was "not able to sit or get out of bed". Then on the next day:

> he suddenly left his bed and appeared very bright, claiming he was free of all pain and feelings of sickness. He intended to leave the hospital the next day. A quarter of an hour after the attending physician left him, he fell unconscious and died within a few minutes.

The front of his brain was subsequently found to contain "two pus-filled tissue bags the size of a hen's egg".

Another case involved an 81-year-old Icelandic woman who had displayed symptoms of dementia while living in a retirement home for years. It was reported that despite regular visits from family members "she had neither recognized any of them nor spoken to them" during her final year. But during a visit by her son Lydur, the elderly woman "[s]uddenly sat up, looked him directly in the face, and said, 'My Lydur, I am going to recite a verse to you'". She then recited "clearly and loudly" the verse (which was translated "into unrhymed English by one of the authors"):

> Oh, father of light, be adored.
> Life and health you gave me.
> My father and mother.
> Now I sit up, for the sun is shining.
> You send your light in to me.
> Oh, God, how good you are.

The woman then laid back upon her pillow and was unresponsive until dying about a month later. Thinking this was his mother's work Lydur wrote down the verse and later found out that it was the opening stanza from an Icelandic poet's psalm. This case was similar to several of the reviewed cases in that it exhibited a spiritualized perspective.

A 1990 report on the case of a 5 year old boy was related. The boy had been a coma for three weeks as he lay under the influence of a malignant brain tumor. The boy had reportedly been "almost constantly" in the presence of relatives during that period. Then following the advice of their minister they told the boy that it was ok if he died. Then:

> suddenly and unexpectedly, the boy regained consciousness, thanked the family for letting him go, and told them he would be dying soon. He did in fact die the next day.

An additional case involving Alzheimer's disease had been personally communicated to the authors. The case pertained to an elderly woman who had been sufficiently cognitively-detached for years that "she showed no sign of recognizing her daughter or anyone else". Somehow, though, in the moments before she died "she started a normal conversation with her daughter". The daughter was shocked and was left "utterly confused".

A gross effort to ascertain the commonness of terminal lucidity was described. This involved interviewing nursing home staff and this uncovered that "interviewees from all units reported first hand accounts" of confused seniors "suddenly becoming lucid enough in the last days of life to recognize and say farewell to relatives and carers".

I end this brief look at terminal lucidity with a potentially instructive example from the skeletal realm. Roughly twenty five years ago I was out running in a snowy field and inadvertently stepped in a snow-covered hole. The misstep injured my left big toe. After about a month I visited a podiatrist who promptly took an x-ray of my left foot. He quickly displayed the resulting x-ray image. I promptly pointed to what appeared to be a broken bone and said "busted"? The podiatrist simply nodded his head. I then asked is 'there anything I can do help the situation?'. The podiatrist simply shrugged.

It was a remarkably terse, informative, and ultimately frustrating experience. I had broken one of the imbedded bones beneath the (first and) biggest joint associated with my left big toe (this bone is termed the medial hallucal sesamoid). That bone is apparently difficult to heal and normally offers some regulation of the associated joint. As a result I have opted to wear stiff-soled shoes and more generally avoid bending my big toe backwards (in extension). It would clearly be a miracle if this skeletal flaw were to rectify itself. Additionally, if that correction then inexplicably reversed itself that would constitute a negative miracle.

I suggest that this situation is roughly analogous to the circumstances in which terminal lucidity happens. There has been a physical setback and that would appear to make difficult if not impossible a return to normal functioning. In the case of neural setbacks these normally do not happen instantaneously or in short order (strokes being an exception, though), but it also appears that they tend to get worse over time (although with sustained effort people can overcome some stroke-inflicted losses). So how could neural function return to normal as death approached? Furthermore, how in some cases is this return to normal function a transient affair?

3.a. Initial Taboo Phenomena

I open here with some perspectives on taboo or paranormal research. The findings of such work appear to offer a number of challenges to the scientific vision of life. Such work also has its own collective establishment and following (and perhaps predictably, hype).

In broad ways, Charles T. Tart's 2009 *The End of Materialism* and Rupert Sheldrake's 2012 *Science Set Free* (now apparently re-titled *The Science Delusion*) are reasonable places to obtain paranormal overviews. Tart worked in the field of transpersonal psychology or parapsychology for many years and from that background his book attempts to overturn the position of materialism. Sheldrake, on the other hand, offers a more philosophical take in part coming from his position as kind of an excommunicated (and rather curious) scientist. Tart's book is centered on paranormal research, while Sheldrake's goes beyond the paranormal front to consider quite a range of alternative topics. I start here with comments based on Sheldrake's fine *Science Set Free*.

Rupert Sheldrake's first, and I think most basic message, is on the rigidity found in the scientific establishment, including its fixation on materialism/physicalism. Sheldrake attempts to communicate that fixation as well as the idealization-prone contemporary following it has generated. To this end Sheldrake included the following characterization of science from the entertainer Ricky Gervais:

[s]cience seeks the truth. And it does not discriminate. For better or worse it finds things out. Science is humble. It knows what it knows and it knows what it doesn't know. It bases its conclusions and beliefs on hard evidence - evidence that is constantly updated and upgraded. It doesn't get offended when new facts come along. It embraces the body of knowledge. It doesn't hold onto medieval practices because they are tradition [Sheldrake 2012b, p.27].

Sheldrake responded to this take by politely calling it "hopelessly naive" in that it implies "scientists as open-minded seekers of truth, not ordinary people competing for funds and prestige, constrained by peer-group pressures and hemmed in by prejudices and taboos [i.e., the default human condition]". I think that such naive characterizations are quite common and suggest Gervais' quote offers a nice backdrop to this book.

Continuing, even in my regular science readings over the years - including *Scientific American*, *New York Times*' science coverage, and also *Union of Concerned Scientists*' literature - there appears to be a strong tendency to view science in an idealized way. Let me suggest that on the other hand, if you want critical self-appraisals (as well as some humor), you are much more likely to find them in sports literature.

One of the distinguishing features of *Science Set Free* is the historical perspective that it provides on the workings of modern science. This includes a number of excellent quotes. Beyond his concentrated coverage of psychic phenomena, though, his book doesn't even address the possibility of life after death. It does, though, consider such taboo questions as "Are the Laws of Nature Fixed?", "Is Matter Unconscious?", as well as "Is All Biological Inheritance Material?" (the latter describes his take on genetics' missing heritability situation). *Science Set Free* appears to be carefully done and it is certainly a good read for those interested in broadening their perspective.

Elsewhere Rupert Sheldrake did make a point of seriously investigating the hypothesis that pet dogs somehow know their owners are coming home [Sheldrake 2011] (this was also briefly touched on in *Science Set Free*). But unless you have some significant intellectual investment in denying such a possibility, would you really care about this claim? Would dog owners love and appreciate their dogs more if it were evident that these pets inexplicably knew when their owners were coming home? What is of perhaps more importance is that Sheldrake follows thru in his appendix to recount his experiences with skeptics, including the Amazing Randi. Pet dogs may inexplicably know when their owners are coming home, but as Sheldrake notes, skeptics appear to have little interest in reading the associated reports. In Randi's case he personally acknowledged to Sheldrake that his publicized debunking efforts of the dog investigations in fact didn't happen [Sheldrake 2011, pp.314-5]. Additionally, in its coverage of psychic phenomena *Science Set Free* also describes other exchanges that Sheldrake had with skeptics and scientists including Richard Dawkins. Skeptics and scientists may project certainty with regards to the status of materialism, but it appears that they rarely bother to investigate challenges to it and thus are quite limited at defending it. Sheldrake also included some third person assessments of those exchanges [Sheldrake 2012b, pp.253-7].

Moving along to Charles Tart's large *The End of Materialism* where there are a lot of coverage on paranormal phenomena. The book focuses on what Tart considers to be the "big five" which are telepathy, clairvoyance, precognition, psychokinesis, and psychic healing. Tart concludes that from many rigorous experiments, as well as spontaneous phenomena, it is reasonable to conclude that:

> humans [are] beings who are more than just their physical bodies, beings who can sometimes communicate mind to mind, sometimes clairvoyantly know the state of the physical world,

sometimes predict an inherently (by physical laws) unpredictable future, sometimes affect physical objects by thought and intention alone, and sometimes affect, for the better, other biological systems, as in psychic healing [Tart, p.291].

Tart then suggested that these big five phenomena provide "glimpses of mind operating in this larger [spiritual] reality" [Tart, p.291]. The remaining topics in the book Tart characterizes as "maybes", and these include out-of-body experiences, near-death experiences, postmortem survival, and reincarnation.

Tart's book tries to tie these phenomena to a larger significance, in particular, that these provide evidence of our spiritual nature. I found this at times to be difficult to read as Tart seems to do too much hand-holding. This includes an excessive amount of explaining on topics like how science is supposed to work; about the differences between religion and spirituality; and about the nature of our psychological tendencies and biases (Steven Pinker also tends to do this). I suggest that if the paranormal examples sufficiently contradict materialism then that should suffice in ending materialism (although don't expect scientists and skeptics to acknowledge anytime soon). Making the larger connection to a deeper spiritual vision, though, is not easy given the rare and/or small scope of most paranormal phenomena. Given his experimental background in parapsychology, Tart seems to unfortunately undervalue some of the truly amazing singular psychic phenomena in favor of much more modest - albeit controlled - laboratory observations.

A problem I suggest in Tart's selection of the "big five" - and parapsychology in general - can be clarified with an analogy. Imagine if you will that some prominent scientists were to come out and claim that our sense of humor or our tempers, are simply illusions. This could be quite an entertaining development, with at least the former conjecture probably being utilized in standup comedy. The thing about these qualities - our tempers and sense of humor - is that they are gross everyday phenomena and as such they are self-evident (although in the posited scenario I still imagine that some academics would stand by the prominent scientists' denial position). Conversely, by focusing on the experimentally-observed big five, Tart's argument about ending materialism then depends on marginal phenomena which appear to have small net significance. The acceptance of such phenomena might eventually produce nightmares for some materialists (and nominally end the reign of materialism), but it could arguably do little to change our perspective on life. Ideally, some of the well-supported examples could then over time gain general acceptance; scientists and skeptics might retreat to a so-rare-who-cares stance; and inevitably some intellectuals would feel compelled to wheel in some kind of esoteric physics-based explanations (likely involving quantum mechanics which paranormal researchers already routinely do).

Tart's big book does eventually include some singular breakthrough-type events. But for a more straightforward look I next turn to the work of an outsider, Elizabeth Mayer.

3.b. More Taboo, Mostly from Elizabeth Mayer's Accounts

A pretty large set of paranormal challenges to materialism was nicely presented in Elizabeth L. Mayer's *Extraordinary Knowing: Science, Skepticism, and the Inexplicable Powers of the Human Mind* [Mayer]. Mayer's book resulted from her investigation into paranormal phenomena and its collision with her "rational" psychoanalyst's background. Her regular work had included positions in the psychiatry department at the University of California Medical Center, San Francisco, and also as an associate clinical professor of psychology at the University of California at Berkeley.

Elizabeth Mayer's investigations into paranormal phenomena had been initiated by some remarkable help she had received while attempting to recover her daughter's stolen harp.

Following up on a friend's suggestion, Mayer had in desperation contacted an Arkansas man who worked as a dowser. Her initial phone calls to the man went as follows:

> "Give me a second," he said. "I'll let you know if it is still in Oakland [where it was stolen]." He paused, then: "Well, it's still there. Send me a street map of Oakland and I'll locate the harp for you." After overnighting the man a map she got a call back two days later. "Well, I got that harp located," he said, "It's in the second house on the right on D— Street, just off L— Avenue" [Mayer, pp.2-3].

Mayer then went on to locate that intersection and subsequently placed flyers offering a reward in the two-block area surrounding the specified house. Three days later she got a phone call from a man who claimed to have seen the missing harp in the possession of a neighbor. After some further calls Mayer arranged to have a meeting at which she was able to recover the stolen harp.

Continuing with some of Mayer's subsequent experiences with psychics (or intuitives). After the over-the-phone success in locating her daughter's harp, Mayer wanted to check out other individuals with purported psychic abilities. She then phoned a woman in Cape Cod, Deb Mangelus [pp.43-5]. After giving Mangelus her first name Mayer then held back any other information. Mangelus, though, after a brief pause started into some commentary:

> "[y]ou're in the middle of a decision. There are two women involved. They're very different. One is fiery, playful, someone you can always have fun with. She has trouble with words. Maybe she's not always reliable. Fire is a big part of the image; I see the two of you holding hands around a campfire." She pauses. "The other woman is different - really different. She's very responsible. Dutiful. Orderly.

> The funniest thing is happening. ... I keep seeing her hands and they're clasped in her lap. I simply can't get her to unclasp her hands.".

Mangelus' commentary provided a jolt to Elizabeth Mayer. She had in fact been struggling with a hiring decision. It came down to two female candidates for a managing director position in an arts organization. Here is some of Mayer's reflective commentary:

> [Mangelus's] description of each woman struck me as unbelievably accurate. I'd liked the first woman a lot. She seemed like she would be enormous fun to work with, though her writing samples were terrible and I wondered how she'd handle details. I'd been less drawn to the other woman. She seemed great on details, but I doubted if she ever got excited about what she was doing. She struck me as boring. Even more to the point was this: The second woman had managed to sit through our entire two-hour interview holding her hands firmly clasped in her lap. At the time I had repeatedly wondered to myself, "How can anyone possibly keep her hands so solidly clasped for so long?".

Mayer additionally pointed out that the first woman (the enthusiast) had such fiery red hair that as she exited the interview Mayer had joked to her, "*Now* I know what fiery red hair really means!"

Such experiences amazed Mayer and she thus repeatedly concluded that "*this changes everything*". It certainly strains any conceivable physical explanation that I can think of, but I have a problem with "*everything*" beginning with the possibility that it may not have helped her with the hiring decision. Nonetheless, Mayer went on to conclude that through her usage of the intuitive Mangelus, and despite telling her "nothing or as close to nothing as I could consciously manage", this woman revealed insight:

> that made me feel that she saw my life with a clarity my closest friends couldn't match, things I knew but hadn't yet recognized that I knew. They rang extraordinarily true and were also extraordinarily important. She pinpointed the central dilemmas, choices, situations, and desires in my life. [She] was somehow breaking every mold I recognized about how people achieve insight about themselves. She *knew* me. And I couldn't begin to explain how.

Her subsequent experiences with another psychic, Ellen Todd, were also reported on. Here again Mayer offered no verbal introduction even though this interaction was done in person. One notable intuition was offered with regards to the very serious nature of one of Mayer's daughters. The psychic offered an explanation for this girl's demeanor based on a very difficult experience that had occurred in a previous life. Mayer was not willing to accept that explanation, but the awareness of this unusually serious demeanor and the associated challenge impressed her. Mayer concluded the session by giving Todd five names and asking her for any insight into the named individuals (among whom Mayer was considering collaboration). The psychic went on to comment on four of them but was stymied on one. Todd commented that it happens sometimes that I "simply couldn't find them". Mayer later went on to check on that person and it turned out they had unexpectedly died two weeks earlier.

In a final look at the work of psychics, I consider Elizabeth Mayer's report on her interaction with John Huddleston [Mayer, pp.51-2]. Huddleston provided Mayer with some of his impressions about her family. Mayer wrote about his commentary, "I told John that he had been right on a lot of things, but was totally off the mark about one person". Of that person Mayer wrote, "[i]t was simply impossible for that person would do what John told me he'd been doing". Huddleston, though, responded in a "relaxed and easy fashion" that "he could sometimes be wrong", but, "he'd stick to his guns on this one". Mayer went on to write:

> [t]welve days later, I received the news. Everything that John had told me turned out to be accurate. I was as stunned as the rest of the family - but they didn't have to contend with the fact that someone had told me all about it twelve days earlier.

Another remarkable insight that would seem to suggest that at least for some people (perhaps a very tiny minority), under certain circumstances, they can obtain information in ways that defy any normal explanation.

Another interesting aspect in Mayer's coverage was her inclusion of psychics' explanations for their paranormal abilities. They seemed humble and matter of fact about the subtle state they feel facilitates their intuitive insights. Inaccuracies were acknowledged as possible. Huddleston' explanation stood out in part for its optimism. He said his mind state during a reading was:

> *relaxed focus*, that is the best way to describe it. There's calm, clarity, and a receptive quality. There's also a physical component, and by that I mean I'm physically centered and grounded within myself, not drifty and discorporate. I'm in communication with the client, the barriers are down, and they are very easy to see, but I don't merge with them in order to read them. This is not an out-of-body experience, in fact my state of mind is surprisingly down to earth and ordinary.

Huddleston went on to second the claim that such psychic readings are "surprisingly ordinary" and "[i]n fact most people use aspects of this state of mind in their daily lives without realizing it". I disagree with this point and suggest that if this were true it should be self-evident as with our sense of humor. These really do appear to be remarkable and unusual abilities.

I change over now to a different kind of phenomenon also discussed in *Extraordinary Knowing*. This one shows up in Mayer's chapter on remote viewing research and includes some practical insights. The remote viewing research work considered here was done at Stanford Research Institute (SRI) and it had been initiated via some fallout from a visit to SRI by an artist and psychic, Ingo Swann. During that visit Swann had proceeded to remotely manipulate a number of shielded instruments and generally astonish some personnel at SRI. His initial remote viewing exercise helped establish funded parapsychology research work at SRI. The funding eventually totaled 20 million dollars for 24 years worth of work. It initially came from the Central Intelligence Agency (CIA) [Mayer, p.106].

Some of the remote viewing experiments as one resident physicist put it, "were anything but ordinary and [they] just blew our minds" [p.108]. One example of a remote viewing exercise appeared to fail in a large way. Latitude and longitude coordinates had been given separately to two men (Swann and a retired policemen, Pat Price), both of whom claimed to possess some remote viewing abilities. Those coordinates were seemingly of a mundane rural location. The viewers, though, went on to independently discuss an elaborate, nearby underground facility which they assumed was the intended viewing target. As it turned out the SRI people later found out from the CIA that right next to the coordinate-designated location was a "highly sensitive underground government installation". One of the viewers even got the classified installation's name right.

Another remote viewing example considered by Mayer was national security-inspired and involved a recruit from the ranks of the U.S. Army Intelligence and Security Command, Joe McMoneagle [pp.116-7]. McMoneagle had been very successful in his military career and from answers in a series of interviews he was somehow judged to have good remote viewing potential. Joe McMoneagle in fact turned out in his new intelligence career to "produce masses of data that were really hot and totally inexplicable by ordinary means".

In one example McMoneagle was given told coordinates in the Soviet Union. Those coordinates unbeknownst to McMoneagle (and likely almost everyone else on the planet) were where an enormous building was. Seemingly in the middle of nowhere that building had just come to the attention of U.S. intelligence officials. McMoneagle's:

> immediate response was that [the coordinates] identified a very cold wasteland with an extremely large industrial-looking building that had enormous smokestacks, not far from a sea capped with thick cap of ice. Later we found out the location was Severodvinsk on the White Sea.

After noting his initial success, the investigators gave McMoneagle a surveillance photo of the big building and asked him to try to see inside the building. Here is an excerpt from McMoneagle's retrospective account:

> I spent some time relaxing and emptying my mind. Then with my eyes closed, I imagined myself drifting down into the building, passing downwards through its roof. What I found was mind-blowing. The building was easily the size of two or three huge shopping centers, all under a single roof ...

> In giant bays between the walls were what looked like cigars of different sizes, sitting in gigantic racks. ... Thick mazes of scaffolding and interlocking steel pipes were everywhere. Within these were what appeared to be two huge cylinders being welded side to side, and I had an overwhelming sense that this was a submarine, a really big one, with two hulls.

At that time the US intelligence community felt that the Soviets were building a new type of assault ship in the building. After describing some other remote observations, McMoneagle added:

> I did a detailed drawing of the submarine, adding dimensions, as well as noting the canted[/slanted] [ballistic missile] tubes, indicating eighteen to twenty in all.

McMoneagle even came up with an accurate launch date (January) for the submarine. The subsequent January's surveillance photos revealed a large twin-hulled submarine on the move. It roughly matched Joe's description, including the presence of twenty canted missile tubes. A look at Wikipedia offers corroboration on length, 574 feet, and also provides some insane details like the fact that each of the twenty missiles carried 10 independently targetable nuclear warheads. The name of this Soviet submarine model was Typhoon.

An amazing and seemingly sincere report of "extraordinary knowing". The presence of such skills could certainly be of interest in the foreign intelligence area. Also at one point Joe McMoneagle described the frightening feelings that came with performing his remote viewing exercises, but these might have been modest next to what an actual spy on location could have expected.

I close this segment here with a few comments. In other writings I have given some of my own experiences but such experiences probably are relatively common (and perhaps this taboo discussion is getting too long). Continuing, if psychic abilities are real and somehow consistent with the scientific model then that would appear to require a basis in our nervous system and also have some DNA and evolutionary support. I suggest that the hegemony of scientific materialism has reduced the communication of such mysterious occurrences. I think such occurrences are probably not uncommon but that they tend to be shelved in the modern intellectual world. For a published example, interested readers can see the late author Peter Matthiessen's account of his remarkable premonition of the coming death of his wife. It is given in the second chapter of his book, *Nine-Headed Dragon River* [Matthiessen]. Additionally, for those wishing to see a fuller assessment of the marginalization of psychic phenomena you might see [Sheldrake 2012b, pp.231-59].

But on the other hand, I also have doubts about the apparent long term abilities of some psychics like those reported on in *Extraordinary Knowing*. I tend to think that psychic abilities are obviously inexplicable, show up occasionally, but might just be blips if you will. Conceivably, though, a few people might experience a sustained run of them. But I suspect that such blips reflect a fragile phenomena and as such shouldn't be expected. One possible exception is that some traditions suggest that some sustained spiritual practices can boost the likelihood of ESP occurrences (although they tend to be viewed as distractions at least from my exposure to Buddhist literature). A big but exceptional scenario might be found with claims of miracles found in the accounts of prominent religious figures (including perhaps a contemporary one [Levine]). A small meditation-related example can be found with Matthiessen's aforementioned premonition which happened during a mediation retreat. But even if accurate these appear to be detours from the traditional goals of religious/spiritual life (see Chapter 3).

3.c. Taboo Follow-up from Mark Gober's Upside Down Book

I add a little more taboo commentary this based on a 2018 book, An End to Upside Down Thinking: Dispelling the Myth That the Brain Produces Consciousness, and the Implications for Everyday Life [Gober]. The book appears to have been carefully researched and written by an outsider, Mark Gober. It represents Gober's survey of paranormal research topics and I found it to be a good review book. It seems analogous to Mayer's Extraordinary Knowing, although missing the personal connections found therein and also missing an acknowledgment to Mayer's book (this unfortunately could be typical as her book from my readings tends to be routinely overlooked).

Before getting to a few paranormal highlights I feel compelled to open with a general criticism, though. Gober's most general point - which he opens the book with - is that there is a case for arguing materialism in reverse. That is, as given in his caption for an alternative pyramidal depiction of reality:

> consciousness is fundamental and everything else (e.g., physical matter and the universe ... and even brains) come from, and is experienced within consciousness [Gober, p.xxi].

Gober appears to have gone from some remarkable and credible paranormal phenomena and then concluded that consciousness creates "everything else". This is a gigantic extrapolation. Why not simply let these mysteries be communicated as is and then readers can wonder about them? And how would concluding that consciousness creates everything change a person's mindset? Someone might then begin pursuing positive thinking in a big way (and good luck with that).

On somewhat of a parallel if you read physicists' and/or astronomers' assessment of the significance of their own usually speculative and often remote research topics, you can find somewhat of an analogous overreach. This tends to show up at the end of *Scientific American* physics articles. Gober's overreach also overlaps with that found in other paranormal researchers' big picture assessments. Such assessments tend to involve taking what seems to be casual comments by physicists on the nature of reality (usually based on quantum speculation and perhaps some alcohol consumption) and taking them too seriously.

But aside from this oversized general hypothesis Gober did a nice job of laying out some of the paranormal results. One notable thing that Gober included was copies of official declassified U.S. government assessments on SRI's remote viewing work. In one of these documents a science panel consisting of Dr. Donald M. Kerr (Director of Los Alamos National Laboratory), Dr. Fred Zacharaison (physics professor at California Institute of Technology), and W. Ross Adey (Chief of Staff, Research Division, Veterans Administration Hospital) produced a "Principal Findings" document stating (in capital letters) that:

IMPLICATIONS ARE REVOLUTIONARY

MERITS CONTINUED FUNDING IN THE NATIONAL INTEREST
EVIDENCE TOO IMPRESSIVE TO DISMISS AS MERE COINCIDENCE
LACK OF PHYSICAL MODEL DOES NOT PRECLUDE EXISTENCE
INITIATE A FIVE-TO-TEN YEAR PROGRAM
INVOLVE ADDITIONAL LABS [pp.71-2].

Another positive conclusion came from the prominent physicist, Freeman Dyson. It is located in *Extraordinary Knowing'* preface and there Dyson suggested that "ESP is real but belongs to a mental universe that is too fluid and evanescent to fit within the rigid protocols of controlled scientific testing" [Mayer, p. xi]. Additionally, Dean Radin in his book *Real Magic* also presents some similar declassified assessments [Radin, pp.218-20].

While the evidence for such extraordinary phenomena appears to be strong, the denial by the scientific establishment is easily a match. Underneath that denial is apparently a firm belief that physicists couldn't be wrong in their general assessment of the universe. That assessment has led physicists to draw some remarkable conclusions. For example, Sean Carroll for one concluded in a blog entry that everything simply consists of 'atoms and the void', and in another case Michio Kaku has apparently dedicated his career to identifying a "1 inch equation" to explain everything [Carroll; Kaku]. Intellectually enforcing the resultant materialism/determinism appears to be the job of skeptics and Gober discussed an example involving the reign of a group of skeptics at Wikipedia.

I close here with two remote viewing examples given in *An End to Upside Down Thinking*. The first involved efforts by the government to locate a downed Soviet Tupolev-22 bomber aircraft in Africa. Satellites could not find the bomber so eventually a remote viewing request led Joe McMoneagle to attempt to find it. In the words of physicist Russell Targ:

> Joe was given a large map of Africa on which he could try to match and record his mental pictures as they emerged. The first thing that he saw on his mental screen was a river flowing north. Working with his eyes alternately open and closed, he followed the river until it flowed between some rolling hills. After a half-hour's work, he drew a circle on the map and said the plane was between the river and a little village shown by a dot. Within two days, the TU-22 was found by our ground forces within the circle that Joe had drawn [Gober, p.66].

President Jimmy Carter later acknowledged the success of this remote viewing operation in a speech to Emory College in 1995 [Gober, p.66].

The second interesting remote viewing exercise occurred in law enforcement. After presenting a report suggesting that there had been some remote viewer usage in about one hundred police departments in the United States, Gober provided an example related to the Patrica Hearst kidnapping. His account begins when:

> [t]he Berkeley [California] police contacted the Stanford Research Institute, asking for psychic assistance on the matter. [Pat] Price was a remote viewer in the program at Stanford and was [willing] to help. His initial psychic impression was that the kidnappers did not want money, and instead, the kidnapping was political in nature. The police showed Price hundreds of unlabeled mug shots, and he picked out three ... Price noted that one of the men "recently had his teeth pulled out at the dentist without anesthesia, relying instead on self-hypnosis".
>
> Two days later, the kidnappers contacted the police, and, as Price predicted, they claimed that they didn't want money; instead they wanted food for the poor. Eventually, police determined that the three men Price picked out were indeed three of the men in this group. Police even confirmed Price's story about the kidnapper's dental incident [Gober, p.207].

This viewing by Price was performed about 50 miles away from the kidnapper's location. Additionally, in Elizabeth Mayer's book it was pointed out that prior to his enlistment with SRI, Price had been a policeman in Burbank, California. Price claimed to have utilized what he termed "ESP" during his career and also that it had led to "some of his most spectacular successes as a police commissioner" [Mayer, p.109].

4. Transgender Children

Some individuals appear to strongly identify with the opposite gender and this identification can show up when they are very young. This isn't a moral issue but it can raise big challenges for the affected individuals. One way and another as human beings we tend to groove into habits and routines, and some of these of course are gender-based. It can be a frustrating situation for an affected individual in their having to live out of synch with their body-type.

Of note here is that I am addressing the profound, innate or early-onset transgenderism. The recent and much more prevalent transgenderism will not be discussed here.

This phenomena is not that uncommon and I have seen adults who have habituated to dressing like the opposite gender. I also have encountered women who although they don't cross-dress, psyche-wise do appear to be like men. The intellectual question here is how could this happen? One transgender study found that among the subset of transgender people that have undergone sex-change surgery (or transitioned) many "knew that they had been born into the wrong gender from childhood" [Landau]. An explanation from the scientific perspective would seem to require some kind of mutation which resulted in an individual whose brain was committed to identifying as the opposite gender, and also somehow being precociously inclined towards the associated agenda.

From an article in the *New York Time Magazine* here is part of a description of a 3 year old:

> he insisted on wearing gowns even after preschool dress-up time ended. He pretended to have long flowing hair and drew pictures of girls with elaborate gowns and flowing tresses. By age 4, he sometimes sobbed when he saw himself in the mirror wearing pants, saying he felt ugly [Padawer].

Such behaviors can present challenges for parents. As one father put it, "I didn't know how to be the father of a girl inside a boy's body".

Additionally, one eight year old's self assessment found in Andrew Solomon's *Far From the Tree* contained [Solomon 2012, pp.604-5]:

> I'm a girl and I have a penis. They [her parents] thought I was a boy until I was six. I dressed like a girl. I said, 'I'm a girl.' They didn't understand for the longest time.

That assessment went on to look ahead (after considering possible fixes for their penis problem) and state:

> [w]hen I'm a mommy I'll adopt my babies, but I'll have boobies to feed them and I'll wear a bra, dresses, skirts, and high-heeled shoes.

Are such behaviors plausible in terms of evolution and in particular as a function of DNA specifications?

The author Solomon described an incident following a transgender workshop. One anxious dad approached the workshop presenters with the question, "[b]ut what if he changes his mind?". One of the presenters came back with, "[y]ou just explained how he told you on the changing table at two that he was a girl, and that message hasn't changed in thirteen years". Solomon went on to add that it took the presenters "about ten minutes to bring this man around to an acceptance he had been unable to achieve for over a decade" [Solomon 2012, p.641]. One trans child had told his parents at age 15 months, "I'm not a boy. I'm a girl". This child then went on to request a Barbie doll at age two. Another trans girl at age two had a favorite pastime of wearing their mother's "red high heels, a towel on his head for hair, and anything he could drape as a sari" [p.662].

The difficulties facing such trans kids, including an increase risk of suicide attempts, certainly provide some incentive for activism. Solomon claimed out that "[m]ore than of half trans people are rejected by their families", and "even in families with some acceptance, it often comes from only one parent" [Solomon 2012, p.645]. Perhaps, though, this situation has improved over the last decade or so due to increased awareness.

A 2017 *Scientific American* article, "When Sex and Gender Collide", by Kristina R. Olson provided a more science-framed overview of the trans situation [Olson]. Olson stated that:

> when predicting their identities in the future, trans girls see themselves becoming women and trans boys feel that they will be men, just as other girls and boys do. Even when we present children with more indirect or implicit measures of gender identity - the measures that assess reaction times rather than children's more explicit words and actions - we have found that trans girls see themselves as girls and trans boys see themselves as boys, suggesting transgender identities are held at lower levels of conscious awareness.

On gender-oriented behaviors, Olson wrote that:

> [t]he degree of their preferences for stereotypical clothes, as well as their tendency to prefer to befriend those of their self-identified gender and the degree to which they see themselves as members of their gender group, is statistically indistinguishable from their peers' responses on the same measures throughout the childhood years.

Olson added an additional conclusion that:

> [a]ll of this research combines to show that transgender identities in even very young children are surprisingly solid and consistent across measures, contradicting popular beliefs that such feelings are

fleeting or that children are simply pretending to be the opposite gender.

This is a life-challenging dynamic as well as a science-challenging one too. Whatever prevailing intellectual beliefs might be, as a parent of such a child you have an opportunity to come to your own conclusions and that personal understanding might be the best guide.

5. Hyperthymesia

I now turn to another interesting challenge. A 2014 *Scientific American* article, "Remembrance of All Things Past" [McGaugh and LePort], reported on the amazing autobiographical memories observed in a number of individuals. The associated syndrome is called hyperthymesia. That article opened with an excerpt from an e-mail that the author James McGaugh had received from a woman named Jill Price:

> As I sit here trying to figure out where to begin explaining why I am writing you ... I just hope somehow you can help me. I am 34 years old, and since I was 11 I have had this unbelievable ability to recall my past ... I can take a date, between 197[6] and today, and tell you what day it falls on, what I was doing that day, and if anything of great importance ... occurred on that day I can describe that to you as well.

The authors, James McGaugh and Aurora LePort, then followed up and extensively tested Price's recall of events and her memory was eventually proved faulty in one case - the day of the week of one of the previous 23 Easters (and Price happens to be Jewish). Additionally, she "corrected the book of milestones for the date of the start of the Iran hostage crisis at the U.S. embassy in 1979". During the tests she:

correctly recalled that Bing Crosby died at a golf course in Spain on October 14, 1977. When asked how she knew, she replied that when she was 11 years old, she heard the announcement of Crosby's death over the car radio when her mother was driving her to a soccer game.

Price demonstrated an "immediate recall of the day of the week for any date in her life after she was about 11 years old". On the other hand, she also "has trouble remembering which of her keys go into which lock" and moreover "does not excel in memorizing facts by rote". The remainder of the article chronicled the authors' subsequent confirmation of similar abilities in about 50 people. These outstanding memories were found to be "highly organized in that they are associated with a particular day and date" and that it occurred "naturally and without exertion".

To try a relevant exercise here readers might pause and write down a year from the last decade. Next, you can then write down a month and also a date in that month. In so doing you have specified a day that occurred in the last 10 years. Perhaps something like April 21, 2018. Now for the interesting part - try figuring out which day of the week that day occurred on (you can go easy here and skip trying to recall the associated global and personal events). Even such day of the week deciphering appears very implausible in a "naturally and without exertion" biological fashion.

This extraordinary hyperthymesia phenomenon should have an explanation and given its effortless nature, scientifically that implies a DNA basis. This would mean that such people should have a specific DNA pattern that somehow fell out of evolution that allows them to effortlessly recall their lives and significant events, in a date and day-of-the-week fashion. This point is followed up by the authors, but they didn't acknowledge the scientific jaw-dropping implications of this phenomenon. This is a little introduction to the kind of miracles expected of

DNA and evolution (not to mention brains). I suggest that such miracles would be very implausible even if - as will be shown not to be the case - the last 20 years or so of scouring our DNA had found significant connections between DNA and innate behavioral characteristics.

I suggest the punchline here, though, is that very few people - certainly amongst those educated - appear to doubt the underlying *its-in-the-DNA* logic of genetics and evolution, and thus the prevailing logic of life.

6. Multiple Personality Disorder

The condition of multiple personality (or dissociative identity) disorder will now be considered here via an in-depth *Scientific American* article, "A New Therapy for Multiple Personality Disorder Helps a Woman with 12 Selves", by Rebecca J. Lester [Lester]. Secondarily, interested readers can find an online lengthy follow-up discussion with Lester [Fischman et al]. Lester is a licensed social worker specializing in trauma and one of the challenges she has worked with is personality disorders. Lester is also a "cultural anthropologist with expertise in the intersections of culture and mental health". The patient her article chronicled was described with the fictitious name, Ella. Here from Lester's opening paragraph was an introduction:

> [s]he was sitting comfortably in a chair, her hands folded, her back straight and her feet flat on the floor. There was no dramatic change, no shuddering or twitching. But then I saw it: in slight shift in how she held her body. Her face softened almost imperceptibly. I heard it, too: her voice sounded different, pitched just a teeny bit higher than usual, with a new singsong quality. At first I found it curious. As it continued, I felt a growing sense of unease. Acting on a hunch, I asked her how old she was. "I'm seven," she said. Ella was 19.

Ella had been referred to Lester by a professor of hers. Lester and Ella met and worked together two and then three times a week. That collaboration was described as having lasted 4 and a half years. Ella had originally been described as needing help with complex post-traumatic stress disorder. She had experienced "long-term, severe abuse by a trusted religious leader". As a result she had had flashbacks, anxiety, nightmares, and was involved with self-harm. Standing out more, though, was that she:

> regularly missed pockets of time. She 'spaced out' unexpectedly, 'waking up' wearing different clothes. She experienced intense thoughts, motions and urges that felt like were coming from someone other than herself.

All together, Lester after many meetings concluded that Ella had multiple personality disorder (MPD). A condition in which there are multiple "personalities that regularly take control of the person's behavior, as well as recurring periods of amnesia". Ella used the term "parts" in referring to her personalities and there were reported to be 12 of them whose ages ranged from two to sixteen. The situation can be very difficult. But it is also believed to be not that rare with global prevalence estimates of around "1 to 1.5 percent of the population." This global recognition could provide some substantial support for an amazing phenomenon.

Each of Ella's parts appeared to have its own name and also collection of memories. They also portrayed "distinctive speech patterns, mannerisms, and handwriting". Some of these parts used words for communication, while other parts "were silent, conveying things through drawings or using stuffed animals to enact scenes". Furthermore amazingly, "[m]ost of the time the different parts were not aware of what was happening when another part was 'out'." This was not surprisingly a recipe for a very "fragmented and confusing existence." As an example, Ella reportedly "would sometimes 'wake up' in the middle of a conversation with someone and realize she was somewhere other than the place in which she last remembered being."

Rebecca Lester reported that MPD is a "highly controversial" diagnosis. I suggest here that anything that challenges scientific materialism - as MPD certainly does - is likely to be controversial, if not simply ignored. Nonetheless the condition as Lester observed, is profound and represents a big challenge. Also it also appears to have had recognition globally which again provides some support for this amazing phenomenon.

Lester reportedly went to great lengths to verify the consistency of Ella's multi-faceted personality and behaviors. Extended fraudulence by Ella would seem to have represented a big personal setback since her parts "would sabotage one another, ruining relationships and threatening her school performance". In a relevant example, Ella reported that two of her more prominent parts, an easy-going 7 year old (Violet) and a demanding 16 year old (Ada), at times came into serious conflict. The older Ada would usually prevail over Violet and as punishment "would sometimes hurt 'the body' by hitting and biting her arms and legs and holding pillow over her face until she passed out, behaviors experienced as a reenactment of the abuse that created her."

Lester then went on to report on her strategy of viewing Ella as consisting of a community. Thus her challenge as a therapist - and agreed upon by Ella - was to attempt to improve the cooperation within that community. Lester also gave an anthropological backdrop and in so doing pointed out that some traditional cultures believed in humans being occupied by multiple souls. For example Lester pointed out that a group in West Africa (the Dahomey) "believed that women had three souls and men had four". She claimed that "the possibility of more than one entity residing in a body at a time is a widespread human belief." I think that such a belief might reflect experiences with MPD or analogous anomalies, but excepting for the routine divisiveness/divisions associated with our competing desires, normal human behavior does not seem compatible with a multiple self interpretation or model. This sincere MPD account is certainly a challenge to interpret scientifically. Rebecca Lester took a stab at this in normalizing Ella's situation by claiming that she isn't that "different from the rest of us, except, that she has barriers between her parts that disrupt the sense of continuous consciousness most of us take for granted." But I don't see how that is realistic. For her parts to have separate identities including memories, speech patterns, and handwriting represents quite a conundrum for any single brain explanation. Functions like handwriting and speech patterns, as neuroscience imagines them, should be somewhat localized in the brain. How could such neural neighborhoods be effectively partitioned to support the distinct features of multiple selves? And how could our evolutionary trek have allowed for something like this?

An additional mystery is how some of the components or parts appear to be frozen in time (or state of development). How could the seven year-old Violet not cognitively age or at least stay crudely consistent with Ella's bodily age and development? An intuitive explanation is that there was somehow an introduction of additional souls (underlying me's) and that they then struggled to make appearances and/or influence Ella's existence. The following anomalous behavioral phenomenon also fits that pattern in a more straightforward way.

7. Personality Changes Following Heart Transplants

A number of reports have suggested that in some cases heart transplant recipients received more than a functioning heart [Leister; Verny; Pearsall et al]. In fact the "transfer of personality characteristics from one person to another" following such surgeries has been noted for over 50 years [Leister; Lunde]. These reports in particular suggest that this transference process involves four phenomena: "(1) changes in preferences, (2) alterations in emotions/temperament, (3) modifications of identity, and (4) memories from the donor's life" [Leister]. For simplicity I will largely report on this based on the writeup "Organ Transplants and Cellular Memories" which was published in *Nexus* Magazine [Pearsall et al]. The authors, Paul Pearsall, Gary E. Schwarz, and Linda G. Russek (all PhDs) also authored earlier relevant articles listed in their Endnotes. Further, Pearsall had authored a related book, *The Heart's Code*. Additionally, there have been several follow-up works since, but the *Nexus* article nicely captures the nature of such reports and its cases appear to be regularly cited in later work such as a *Medical Hypothesis* paper [Leister].

The authors introduced their cases along with a suggested explanation-route, cellular memories (which will be consider later). A feature common to a number of the cases is that recipients knew little with regard to the identity of the donor. In all of their cases the recipients had been diagnosed with some form of impending heart failure, but for brevity I removed the associated medical descriptions. I will also forgo Pearsall et al's introduction by directly presenting their Case 4 (there are 10 in all). The donor for Case 4 was black male 17 year-old who had been fatally shot in an apparent drive-by shooting. His mother described his final moments in which after being shot while walking to violin class, he had "hugg[ed] his violin case". He had loved classical music despite being teased by peers, and his mother stated that his teachers were impressed. She further felt "he would have been in Carnegie Hall some day".

The 47 year-old white foundry worker recipient suggested that in the aftermath of the transplant surgery that "I used to hate classical music, but now I love it". Additionally, he added "So I know it is not my new heart, because a black guy from the 'hood wouldn't be into that" and also that "[n]ow it calms my heart". Finally, in the quoted excerpt the foundry employee mentioned that with regard to classical music "I play [i.e., listen to] it all the time".

The recipient's wife pointed out that in addition to socializing now more with black co-workers, her husband was:

> driving me nuts with the classical music. He doesn't know the name of one song and never, never listened to it before. Now he sits for hours and listens to it. He even whistles classical music songs that he could never know. How does he know them? You'd think he'd like rap music or something because of his black heart.

The Case 5 donor had been a 19 year-old woman who had been killed as a result of a car accident. That donor's mom said of the donor/victim that she was a "most loving girl". She had "owned and operated her own health food restaurant and scolded me constantly about not being a vegetarian". Although she was reportedly a bit "[w]ild", she was described by her mom as a "great" kid. Her mother suggested that she had been into "the free-love thing and had a different man in her life every few months". She also claimed that her daughter had been "man crazy" even when she was only a "little girl". When dying the daughter reportedly communicated that she "could feel the impact of the car hitting them" and that she felt it "going through her body".

The corresponding Case 5 recipient was 29 year-old woman who reported that "two things happened" after her transplant surgery. Her first claim was that "I could feel the accident my donor had" in fact "I can feel the impact in my chest", despite her doctor suggesting that "everything looks fine". Her second post-surgery claim was that "I hate meat now", adding that she just "can't stand it" now. She further claimed that "I was McDonald's biggest moneymaker, and now meat makes me throw up" and that when "I even smell it, my heart starts to race". Her doctor was dismissive of this change and suggested "it was due to [her] medicine".

Furthermore, the Case 5 recipient claimed she had effectively had "a gender transplant" as she had no desire to "be with a woman" now. Although she previously had been committed to being gay, after the surgery she found that her new "boyfriend turns" her on but that "women don't". She in fact had gotten engaged to be "married to her boyfriend". The recipient's brother, in addition to confirming the change in dietary preference, also reported that his sister had been "gay and her new heart made her straight". Additionally, the brother reported that the recipient had thrown "out all her books and stuff about gay politics and never talks about it anymore", despite earlier being "militant" on the topic. That brother also added that after previously lecturing about the evils of men, after the surgery she even "talks girl-talk with my girlfriend".

The Case 7 donor was a 3 year-old girl who had died in a tragic accident in the family pool. The tragedy apparently had involved an inattentive babysitter. The only testimony that Pearsall et al obtained was from the recipient's side of the transplant surgery. The recipient's mom claimed that her son didn't know about the donor or how they had died. She reported "that [her son] is now deathly afraid of water", but previously "[h]e loved it". In fact they "live on a lake and he won't go out in the backyard" and he "keeps closing and locking the back door".

That Case 7 recipient was a nine year-old boy who claimed that "he talks to her [the donor] sometimes" and that she "seems very sad" and "very afraid". The boy added that "[s]he says she wishes that parents wouldn't throw away their children" but the nine year-old recipient didn't know "why she would say that". Perhaps consistent with this the recipient's mother pointed out that although her son didn't know about the donor or their death, "we [his parents] do". That mother claimed that the donor's parents had had a subsequent "ugly divorce", and a key point - and likely source of guilt - had been the lack of time spent with their daughter.

The donor for Case 6 was a 14-year-old girl who had died as a result of a gymnastics accident. The mother of the donor spoke in glowing terms about how energetic and fit her daughter had been. She did, though, have an apparent anorexia-like difficulty with food; which despite her active life she had little interest in. Additionally, the donor when embarrassed would emit a "silly little giggle" which "sounded like a little bird".

The associated Case 6 recipient was a 47-year-old man. The recipient's brother claimed that after the surgery the recipient "is a teenager". The brother added that "[h]e's a kid or at least thinks he is a kid" and that while bowling "he yells and jumps around like a fool". The brother also commented that the recipient somehow obtained a "weird" laugh, one sounding like "a girl's laugh". On a final note of some concern, the recipient's brother suggested out that the 47-year-old after surgery "was pretty much nauseous almost all the time". As a result there were subsequently health concerns, including "[h]is doctor" being "concerned about his weight".

The Case 6 recipient claimed that after surgery he felt "like a teenager" and "actually" felt "giddy". He acknowledged that he now "had this annoying tendency to giggle that drives my wife nuts". The recipient also mentioned his subsequent difficulty with eating and feeling nauseous.

Finally, Pearsall et al's Case 10 involved a 34-year-old male donor who had been killed as he tried to arrest a drug dealer. The donor's wife claimed that her husband had died as a result of being shot in the face and that the (un-arrested) suspect's appearance had been described as looking "sort of like some of the pictures [i.e., drawings] of Jesus".

The associated Case 10 transplant recipient was a male 56-year-old college professor and he offered a striking report. He said:

> [i]f you promise you won't tell anyone my name, I'll tell you what I've not told any of my doctors. Only my wife knows. I only knew that my donor was a 34-

year-old very healthy guy. A few weeks after I got my new heart, I began to have dreams. I would see a flash of light right in my face and my face gets real, real hot. It actually burns. Just before that time, I would get a glimpse of Jesus. I've had these dreams and now daydreams ever since: Jesus and then a flash. That's the only thing I can say is something different, other than feeling good for the first time in my life.

The wife of the recipient concurred about the disturbing dreams and also added "God we wish they would stop."

The above seemingly sincere accounts challenge the science's vision of life and of course are amazing. The authors tried to suggest a materialist approach with their hypothesis in which the cells of the donor's heart somehow pass along memories to the transplant recipient. They offered a general and seemingly reasonable concept beginning with "all dynamical systems store information and energy to various degrees". We can sidestep the energy storage point here and instead consider storage of information in the "dynamical systems", which here would be heart cells. Could there be storage of information in such cells? Perhaps yes in a very simple way and thus epigenetic storage mechanisms (involving environmental-induced modifications to the packaging of the DNA strand) might allow such cells to better adapt to changes in blood chemistry. But such storage of information which might help with simple adaptation to physical changes (perhaps in the blood's salinity levels), doesn't seem remotely relevant to the complexity needed to store high level information like the appearance of Jesus or classical music scores.

Additionally, if heart cells offered such a memory capability then why wouldn't there be some analogous phenomena observed with blood transfusions? Blood cells are of course routinely transferred between individuals. Also if hearts are in fact such storage vehicles then why wouldn't there be a deficit in the recipient's memory after the removal of their own heart? Moreover even if somehow the heart cells could store high level information (seemingly redundantly with the brain from a scientific perspective), there still would be the problem of accessing this information in the recipient's body. The neuron-based model of memory is supposed work in a networked associative way. Thus for example, if someone were to mention the movie "Bullitt" to me that reference would likely bring to mind memories of a gritty late sixties crime drama starring Steve McQueen. In turn some other actors in that drama would likely emerge including Robert Vaughn (playing the nasty political figure) and of course the setting, San Francisco. Additionally the very famous car chase scene would certainly come to mind, including its use of a Dodge Charger and a Ford Mustang. The latter might even elicit some personal memories of arguments with other neighborhood kids over the performance of those vehicles since I grew up in a very car conscious family.

That kind of sequence is supposed to reflect an underlying associative structure in which our experience-based memories are somehow neurally connected together. Neuroscience is sure that reflects the many interconnections of many memory-active, distributed neurons. From such a perspective a summation of tiny experience-beget weightings located in the synapses of neurons would somehow make possible the above sketched out unfolding of my memories with regards to "Bullitt". In a more simple example we all can remember personal information (like names) via repetition (my practice is to repeat new names a number of times internally and also to visualize them). The difficulty with the heart hypothesis is simply how could a newly transplanted (presumed memory-bearing) heart get adequately interconnected to effectively come "online" within the recipient's own complex network of memories? This same argument would appear to even also apply to transplanted brain tissue. Adding memory to an electronic computer - via for example an external hard drive - is empirically and conceptually easy. Incorporating external memory within an existing super-interconnected and associatively-built brain network (perhaps visualizable as a big bowl of super thin spaghetti and different people would have different bowls), would likely be very difficult.

Pausing here to add a relevant aside. In his book, *Science Set Free*, Rupert Sheldrake has a chapter entitled "Are Memories Stored as Material Traces" which questions the brain-based vision of memory storage [Sheldrake 2012b, pp.187-211]. Two basic points Sheldrake offered are noteworthy. First, even insiders like Francis Crick have questioned the plausibility of the long term storage of memory in brains. Crick had commented that given the transient nature of molecules within the body this would appear to be a real obstacle to maintaining information over long periods. But more direct evidence challenging the neuronal-model of memory is that there were extensive (and brutal) experiments in which portions of the brains of trained lab animals were removed in an effort to infer the location of memory-relevant structures. These were reported to have failed repeatedly (with trained performance not declining) and this even led a convinced a skeptic in the matter to conclude that "memory is both everywhere and nowhere in particular" [Sheldrake 2012b, p.191].

But beyond these doubts in the brain's potential capacity to maintain memories, there appear to be more basic problems with the heart cellular memory hypothesis. There is more going on in such transplant cases than an unexpected increase in memories, there in fact appears to be three additional categories of changes (see earlier description). When someone gets a big swing in dietary preferences or the inexplicable new attachment to classical music, that would seem to represent more than an increase in personal memories. Additionally, our basic sexual preferences package is supposed to be mostly innate (and thus presumed to have genetic roots), not something conditioned and as such stored in memory.

For a final succinct challenge to the cellular memory hypothesis consider the haunting nightmares that one recipient experienced. According to the authors' theory those would have been based on memories acquired in the shooting death of the donor. But that tragic incident as described likely happened in an instant (certainly the shooting did) and would likely have not provided a basis for any memories. A routine occurrence with serious head-impacting accidents is that memories of the time leading up to the trauma are lost and "likely never will" be obtained [Sheldrake 2012b, pp.196-97; MSKTC 2016].

8. Medium-Based Potential Insights

In the very interesting book by Chris Carter, Science and the Afterlife Experience, there are some remarkable - and in some cases remarkably corroborated - accounts of purported medium-based communications with deceased individuals. For the most part these accounts offer what appears to be a consensus roughly consistent with the traditional life-after-life (or reincarnation) dynamic, with strong moral underpinnings. Those accounts also appear to suggest potential advancement across incarnations - either in terms of species or even planes of existence. Furthermore, the accounts considered by Carter appear to have been communicated with minimal reference to existing religions.

I get started with an introductory quote from a remarkable effort attempting to corroborate medium-based communications. That effort tried to produce a chess game between a contemporary grandmaster (Victor Korchnoi who at that time was ranked third in the world) and a deceased grandmaster [Carter, pp.204-5]. Carter introduced this effort by stating that it:

> began in 1985 when asset-manager and amateur chess player Dr. Wolfgang Eisenbeiss decided to initiate a chess match between living and deceased persons. Eisenbeiss had been acquainted with the automatic-writing medium Robert Rollans (1914-1993) for eight years and trusted his assertion that he

did not know how to play chess and had no knowledge of chess history. Rollans was not paid for his services, and his stated motivation for participation was to provide support for the survival hypothesis.

After being given a list of former grandmasters, Rollans reportedly contacted one of them, Hungarian Gaza Maroczy, who was willing to participate in a medium facilitated match.

The deceased Maroczy was reported to have provided the following motivational statement:

> I will be at your disposal in the peculiar game of chess for two reasons. First, because I also want to do something to aid mankind living on earth to become convinced that death does not end everything, but instead the mind is separated from the physical body and comes up to a new world, where individual life continues to manifest itself in a new unknown dimension. Second, being a Hungarian patriot I want to guide the eyes of the world into the direction of my beloved Hungary a little bit. Both of these items have convinced me to participate in that game with the thought of being at everyone's service.

What stood out in Carter's lengthy account of a medium-connected chess game was first the fine and fitting chess performance Maroczy purported to communicate through the medium Rollans. Maroczy opened weakly as expected - "chess theory has made enormous strides in the way games should be opened" - but as was Maroczy's trademark, he finished with "a strong end-game". Korchnoi and another strong contemporary player felt that the medium-communicated performance was consistent with Maroczy's history. Another impressive point was that via the medium a number of extraordinary details were uncovered and subsequently confirmed about a relatively obscure grandmaster's life. This chess match, by the way, was not an easy affair. Due to health problem with the medium Rollans and also the far-flung lifestyle of the contemporary grandmaster Korchnoi - all in an era prior to omni-electronic communications - the match lasted over 7 years. Rollans in fact died just 19 days after Maroczy resigned the match.

I include the above as a small sample of the remarkable efforts that have been made to corroborate the communications of mediums. Other much more elaborate corroboration efforts purportedly involved the deceased classical scholar Frederic Myers. If such communications are legitimate and meaningful (albeit apparently taboo for many), then it is certainly worth trying to check them with a proverbial fine-tooth comb. Carter and others apparently tried to do that and of additional note such investigative efforts used to be considered legitimate intellectual work. Interested readers can see his book and also be forewarned to bring along an extra helping of patience as the corroboration descriptions (like the efforts themselves) tend to be very involved.

I think that such medium efforts might be analogous to the communications offered by mediums with regards to living people (as discussed in Mayer's *Extraordinary Knowing*). Perhaps akin to such medium efforts, though, I wonder if connections to the deceased are extremely rare. Additionally, this section might also have been placed in the already lengthy taboo phenomena section, as perhaps sub-section 3. D.

I move along now to some descriptions of these medium-based communications. A number of such accounts are considered by Chris Carter in his book. Some of the communications involve notable individuals (as in notable during their recent lives) and some are with relatively anonymous people. A man who identified himself as Rupert Brooke described his death in World War I and his subsequent experiences and confusion. After getting an inkling that something profound had changed - he couldn't see his reflection in a river and apparently being invisible to former colleagues - he added:

> I realized that the reason they couldn't see me was because if my body didn't have a reflection, it couldn't be solid to them. It just couldn't be the same vibration: it couldn't be the same sort of matter. I had to adjust myself to the fact that I had a body which was to all outward appearances the same [to him], and was obviously not a real body from the point of view of Earth. Therefore I was in what I suppose one would term a spiritual body, and yet I was not particularly spiritual. I was puzzled and bewildered [Carter, p.295].

The above period of initial confusion seemed to be common in the reports given. Of note too was that in several cases the purported communicators told about the particular dynamic of the soul exiting the body after death. Some of these reports involved a severing of two "silver cords" between the two bodies and that the cords were deemed to be analogous to an umbilical cord.

One notable communicator, purportedly the philosopher and mathematician Bertrand Russell, found that his initial adjustment came in realizing that:

> [n]ow, here I was, still same I, with capacities to think and observe sharpened to an incredible degree. I felt earth-life suddenly very unreal almost as though it never happened. It took me quite a long time to understand this feeling until I realized at last that matter is certainly illusory although it does exist in actuality; the material world seemed now nothing more than a seething, changing, restless sea of indeterminate density and volume. How could I have thought that that was reality, the last word of Creation to mankind? Yet it is completely understandable that the state in which man exists, however temporary constitutes the passing reality

Science's Dead End, Religions' Opening, and a Restart for Meaning 63

which is no longer reality when it has passed [pp.296-7].

In terms of the big metaphysical picture there were a number of relevant descriptions. The scholar/philosopher Frederic Myers suggested an almost ladder-like progression as souls move up from simple life forms (including plants). In a concise assessment he stated that souls:

> must gather ... numberless experiences, manifest and express themselves in uncountable forms before they attain to completion ... Once these are acquired, [these entities] ... take on divine attributes. The reason, therefore, for the universe and ... the purpose of existence ... [is] the evolution of mind in matter [p.305].

The popularly communicated (through Jane Roberts) figure "Seth" in a summary of his work was thought to believe that:

> each individual consciousness must undergo a long period of training and learning through repeated physical embodiments. Being human is simply one "stage" in this process of development, and when, through related incarnations, this stage is finished, one passes onward to other planes of existence which offer more exalted opportunities for development. The most crucial "lesson" to be learned is karmic or ethical [p.304].

Further in a passage written by the medium Jane Roberts, Seth was claimed to suggest that the (the bracketed content here is included in Carter's original quote):

> responsibility for creation must be clearly understood. [In physical life on earth] ... you are in a soundproof and isolated room. Hate creates destruction in the 'room' and until the lessons are

> learned, destruction follows destruction ... the agonies ... are sorely felt ... you must be taught ... to create responsibly. [Earth life] ... is a training system for emerging consciousness.
>
> "If the sorrows and agonies within your system were not felt as real, the lessons would not be learned ... [It] is like an educational play" [p.305].

In all a huge learning process was conveyed. Helpful strategies were not discussed, though.

A musician named Donald Tovey was reported to communicated that:

> [e]ach and every soul meets here with its just deserts, not because they are dispensed by a presiding deity, but because it is literally true that one reaps what one has sown. If one has endeavored to make the lot of others easier in earth-life and sought to promote the welfare and happiness of one's fellow beings, then one finds oneself in a pleasing environment among congenial companions, and able to adapt without difficulty to the new mode of living. But those who have deliberately deprived others of their material rights and human needs, or have wantonly caused suffering, will find themselves in turn deprived and also imprisoned by their own meanness of outlook. This does not mean that they are trapped for ever in their self-made hell; the moment a soul sees and confesses its past misdeeds and attempts to rectify them, the way opens for it to evolve into the light [p.309].

Among the purported communications from the scholar Frederic Myers was the sense that the default after death experience (at least for humans) could largely involve dream-like projections, and that eventually the soul will want to move beyond this projection business and try to make more sense of their experiences.

Before moving on to some general observations about these communications I consider one potentially significant insight offered. In possible consistency with the aforementioned terminal lucidity, Frederic Myers also reportedly suggested that the:

> very old may, before their passing from earth, in part lose memory or their grasp of facts, their power of understanding. This tragic decay all too often causes the observer of it to lose faith in an After-life. For the soul seems, under such circumstances, merely the brain. This, however, is a false conclusion. The soul, or active ego, has been compelled partially to retire into the double during waking hours because the cord between the brain and its etheric counterpart has either been frayed, or has snapped. The actual life of the physical body is still maintained through the second cord and through any of the threads which still adhere to the two shapes. So the aged, apparently mindless man or woman, is in no sense mindless. He or she has merely withdrawn a little way from you, and has no need for your pity [Carter, p.308].

Myers' communicated message here might be relevant to the amazing rejuvenations seen with terminal lucidity. Instead of requiring an overhaul of long degraded brain-ware, the onset of lucidity might then require only the brief reconnection of something like a cord connecting the brain and the soul [Christopher 2022d]. The "cord" referenced here was also noted in some of the other medium communications. Such purported communications might also hint that brain-based understandings and treatments of Alzheimer's - which have shown very limited return [Kosik; Mosbergen] - might be up against a non-materialist dynamic.

I add here some criticisms, in particular on the prolific communications purportedly from the super-learned Frederic Myers. First, Myers had been a prominent individual; and a friend of the philosopher and psychologist William James; and also had been involved in considerable research questioning the materialism. This could have in part motivated the associated medium communication efforts and subsequent interest in them.

Continuing, Chris Carter covered quite a bit of Myers' purported communications in his book, but the original source is a book by the medium Geraldine Cummins, *The Road to Immortality* (perhaps better titled *On the Immortal Road*). There is an additional book, *Beyond Human Personality*, which I have only read about half of. In these books you certainly get a sense that the communications came from a very serious intellectual (and the medium's own substantial educational background might have contributed to this quality). Further even if the exchanges were genuine sustained attempts at interpersonal communications - and they do appear to have come from sincere efforts - they were still inevitably subject to the limitations of the subtle process along with the biases of the sender and receiver. And in his communications Myers had acknowledged this limitation. One particular frustration I had in reading Myers' purported messages found in Cummins' book, is that at times they are *very* difficult to follow (a glossary would have helped). Myers, in fact, at one point acknowledged that the communication process was difficult and very subtle. It purportedly involves the soul/spirit passing along a message through the medium's "inner mind", which in turn must communicate through their relatively mechanical brain to ultimately get information out to listeners.

An additional layer of frustration I had with those communications was the big picture sense of the trajectory of souls as being at best akin to taking an incredibly long sequence of graduate courses. Somehow as a result of such an extended life-after-life curriculum, souls apparently can work their way up to some form of a Cosmic Philosophy and/or Divinity professorship. Probably chaired, and of course with tenure.

I ended up wondering if the suggested dream-like nature of our initial after-death experience also applied to Myers' extrapolations to a purported seven level (post-death) hierarchy. Perhaps looking for some kind of a consensus among different communicators' visions, and a consensus based on experiences as opposed to speculation towards subsequent potential realms, might be a more reasonable approach for their consideration. In this regard Myer's communications appeared to be over-extrapolated and thus problematic. Myer's also included a prophecy that did not pan out [Cummins, p.xiii] and an endorsement for eugenics [Cummins, p.2].

Furthermore, not mentioned in Carter's presentation is that Myer's communications (as revealed in Cummin's books) were framed within a Christian framework (plus reincarnation and seven levels of existence, and even more including a complicated group soul). Furthermore, Myer's communications that attempted to describe God were very complex. Forget simple ideas like 'God is love', and instead think more like super advanced theology.

Additionally he seemed anchored in a Christianity-versus-Buddhism comparison and decidedly favors Christianity. Christianity at one point was deemed "the religion of fearlessness", while Buddhism was deemed a religion "of certain moral cowardice". A key to this criticism was Myer's conclusion that Buddhism is centered on the eradication or suppression of desire. This does not appear to be accurate as what is sometimes translated as "desire" might better be "craving". Moreover there are schools of Buddhism, in particular one's involving Tantric practices, which point to a potential big role in utilizing desires to facilitate liberation/deeper happiness (which predictably in the West has lead to excessive pursuits) [Yeshe]. Perhaps as a classically trained Western scholar who died 122 years ago he may have had a quite limited exposure to Buddhism.

A much bigger point, though, is - what about the many other religions as well as life-relevant philosophies? Myers may have been exceptionally learned but his purported subsequent communications perspective appears quite limited (albeit interesting).

Furthering an underlying sense of Frederick Myers' perhaps skewed perspective, the opposite of his gist is conveyed through religious or awakening experiences discussed later in Chapter 3. Therein the sense is that some basic understanding is come upon and that this delivers a desirable state (as opposed to finalizing a gargantuan academic-like advancement). For those interested in the considerable (and dense) living writings of Frederick Myers you might see the big academic book, *Irreducible Mind*, which is in large part a tribute to Myers' psychological theories.

Continuing, one of the mysteries associated with life might be that even with significant exposure to a possible after-death realm, we could still be largely anchored in our personal frameworks. The variable nature of near-death experiences appears consistent with this point, see for example ones from a Christian background [Burpo] compared to a Buddhist background [Thondup]. To his credit, though, Myers did include some humble qualifications along with his medium-based communications. It might be best to look for reports of simple post-death dynamics that are consistently presented by a number of communicators.

Additional support perhaps consistent with those medium reports are found elsewhere. One relevant book is psychiatrist Brian Weiss' *Many Lives, Many Masters* which reported on experiences Weiss had with one patient. Neither Weiss nor the patient believed in reincarnation, but their hypnosis-based push back in time (in search of the source of trauma) appeared to uncover memories from earlier (human) lives. Weiss had simply suggested going back further in time and his patient then appeared to vividly recall some striking events, many of them deaths. Weiss also reported that these intense recalls seemed to help the patient resolve some phobias.

9. Our Innate Religious Perspective

An under-appreciated mystery is that we appear to come equipped with some natural religious beliefs or inclinations. Justin L. Barrett in his book, *Born Believers - The Science of Children's Religious Belief*, laid out some of the support for believing that infants tend to innately believe in the existence of God/soul/gods, to possess beliefs in what Barrett termed a "natural religion" [Barrett]. *Born Believers* contained a number of striking examples including ones in which the positions of atheists were rebutted by their young children. As Barrett concluded" [c]hildren are prone to believe in supernatural beings such as spirits, ghosts, angels, devils, and gods during the first four years of life" [Barrett, p.3]. Additionally, he pointed out that:

> Exactly why believing in souls or spirits that survive death is so natural for children (and adults) is an area of active research and debate. A consensus has emerged that children are born believers in some kind of afterlife, but not why this is so [p.120].

This situation was also considered in a popular news site's article. Therein it was stated:

> Olivera Petrovich, an Oxford University psychologist, surveyed several international studies of children aged 4 to 7 and found that the belief in God as a "creator" is "hardwired" in children and that *"atheism* is definitely an acquired position."

> Paul Bloom, a professor of psychology and director of the Mind and Development Lab at Yale University, writes, "The universal themes of religion are not learned... They are part of human nature... Creationism – and belief in God – is bred in the bone" [Wallace].

Justin Barrett included a chapter providing some details associated with our natural religion. This information had been obtained through investigations with young children. These studies suggested that humans are born inclined to hold some beliefs including:

> 1) That there are "[s]uperhuman beings with thoughts, wants, perspectives, and emotions."
> 2) That "[e]lements of the natural world such as rocks, trees, mountains, and animals are purposefully and intentionally designed by some kind of superhuman being(s), who must therefore have superhuman power."
> 3) That "[s]uperhuman beings generally know things that humans do not (they can be super-knowing or super-perceiving, or both), perhaps particularly things that are important for human relations."
> 4) That "[s]uperhuman beings may be invisible and immortal, but they are not outside space and time". They also possess "character, good, or bad."
> 5) That "[l]ike humans, superhuman beings have free will and can and do interact with people, sometimes rewarding and sometimes punishing them."
> 6) That "[m]oral norms are unchangeable, even by superhumans."
> 7) That "[p]eople may continue to exist without their earthly bodies after death" [Barrett, pp.138-9].

Altogether, children seem inclined to believe that there is a significant and unseen additional living realm. That realm is believed to have an overlapping presence with our realm, including a design-oriented aspect.

Barrett went on to carefully qualify the findings about our natural religion. One point he emphasized is that these beliefs are conceptually primitive and that their extension into agreement with more typical religious theology is difficult. It appears that young children (and Barrett suggested adults too) might be naturally religious, but on the other hand they're not inclined to be theological. These remarkable findings were simply placed within the scientific framework, essentially as fallout from evolution and nurture - or " biology plus ordinary environment". Barrett went so far, in fact, as to suggest that research into "systems of the human mind" "make belief in some kind of god almost inevitable" [Barrett, p.20]. This point and Barrett's follow-up, as well as similar content in works like T. M. Luhrmann's How God Becomes Real [Luhrmann 2020], are excellent examples of the hegemony of the materialist vision, since concluding that our innate religious beliefs were the "almost inevitable" outcomes of evolution is frankly ridiculous. I suggest further that the stated findings of the "research into 'systems of the human mind'" are essentially dictated by the assumptions of evolution and materialism.

Barrett, along with other researchers, apparently finds some satisfaction, though, in rebutting the routine anti-religious argument that with regards to religious beliefs, people simply echo what they've been taught. Additionally, he did provide an explanation that he had heard from an Indian man. In Barrett's words that man had explained:

> [T]hat on death, we go to be with God and are later reincarnated. As children had been with God more recently, they could understand God better than adults can. They had not yet forgotten or grown confused and distracted by the world. In a real sense, he explained, children came into this world knowing God more purely and accurately than adults do [Barrett, p.2].

I offer here a couple of related personal examples. One involved a child of about 3 years old walk into an adult conversation I was in and simply say, "There is a God". The child then paused and repeated it. I remember that the conversation I was involved with had dealt with the subject of God and likely involved questioning the existence of God. As far as I know that 3 year old didn't have a supporting religious background and even if they did I doubt it would have mattered. It was quite striking to have a child insist on the existence of God with a conviction perhaps comparable to a declaration of "I need to go to the bathroom".

In an additional incident a child who was about 5 or 6 years matter of factly told me, 'And when we die we go around and find a new mother and go in her tummy and then get born, isn't that right?'. I do know that this child was part of a Muslim family that didn't teach reincarnation. Along with the first case these standout as sincere comments by children that seem to be consistent with our purported natural religion.

I hope more people become aware of our innate spiritual beliefs as they provide a good basis for contemplation of life's possible deeper aspects. For those interested in making sense of religions and their beliefs let me go on to suggest taking a pass on elaborate philosophical and/or astronomical arguments. That we show up as dualists and simple religious believers is probably much more significant to potential credibility than any detours into philosophy or astronomy.

Additionally, I go onto add that the presence of such general beliefs is likely the most important challenge to presented here. If there really is a general deeper dualistic reality - as purported by many religions - that would be the most taboo development from a scientific perspective, and it potentially opens doors to deeper meaning. It obviously also raises many questions.

10. Discussions on Behavioral Challenges

This chapter has attempted to illustrate there are a number of behavioral enigmas facing materialism. The one behavior that could possibly draw some scientific attention is terminal lucidity.

If this happens pretty regularly in institutional settings like nursing homes, it might be difficult for scientists to ignore. There are of course other challenges out there too. In my first book I had a chapter looking at surprising animal behaviors, including interspecies friendships and the wide range of personalities observed among animals [Christopher 2017b]. And for a very taboo example readers might see Gerald Mayer's review of Dean Radin's book *Supernormal* in which he cites a non-esoteric individual (unlike in Radin's book) but simply a German house painter named Anton Peterson (under the stage name, Carry Sunland) and his stunning stage performances [Mayer G]. A further remarkable example was given towards the end of *Extraordinary Knowing* and involved follow-up claims made to Elizabeth Mayer by the Arkansas dowser (the harp-locating Harold). Apparently some people have extraordinary abilities and further appear unimpressed with them.

Another phenomenon that I have neglected here is near-death experiences. These seem to receive enormous coverage and attention, but there could be real limitations as was suggested in a book review of Bruce Greyson's *After*. Much was likely expected of Bruce Greyson's book as he had plenty of research experience in this area (and was also an author of an earlier cited terminal lucidity paper). Anyway, for awhile the most "helpful" review of *After* was a relatively critical one (it gave maybe 2 stars and has since disappeared). The person was interested enough in the topic to have read many books (I have read several including *The Handbook of Near-Death Experiences* for which Greyson was a coauthor [Holden et al]), but that person concluded that there was essentially nothing new in *After*. Additionally, the enormous optimism associated with the popular group, International Association for Near-Death Studies - IANDS, that Greyson is affiliated with - bothered that reviewer.

Although I haven't read *After*, I tend to agree with their criticisms and if significant new findings were presented they would have been widely trumpeted. I suggest the larger neglected point is the basic general question, 'So what?'. If we somehow tend to have positive short-term experiences after death (or in close brushes thereof), then what light does that shed on the big picture? Also, if death is as suggested in much NDE literature a very positive experience, then why is there so much fear of it? Our innate beliefs on the other hand, appear to be general and seem consistent with some form of disembodied existence *before* birth. This could be either a one time pre-birth experience or part of a cyclical phenomenon. Additionally, there might then be an initial period in which that earlier existence stays with us until we have "forgotten or grown confused and distracted by the world". This might then explain some of the 'spaciness' of young kids and perhaps even some of the strange dreams we can have at that age. I will return to this point in the final chapter.

Continuing, it is noteworthy that the type of phenomena in this chapter should have been drawing some academic attention. It is an unfortunate situation that we face now, though, in that credible intellectual challenges (outside of perhaps mathematical ones) are pretty much limited to those deemed acceptable to a materialist perspective.

Perhaps in the future a physicist will write a book in which a subtitle like "The Quest For A Theory of Everything" will reflect a broader appreciation of everything. That subtitle by the way, comes from Michio Kaku's book, *The God Equation*, which as one Amazon reviewer suggested was likely using "God" in order to boost sales. That reviewer also suggested Kaku might likewise have included "Sex" for that purpose.

I close this chapter with a quote about savants from researcher Darnell Treffert:

> no model of brain function, including memory, will be complete until it can fully incorporate and explain this jarring contradiction of extraordinary ability and sometimes permeating disability in the same person. Until we can fully explain the savant, we cannot fully

explain ourselves nor comprehend our full capacities [Treffert, p.xiv].

Chapter 2 - Science's Big Problem - The Missing Heritability

1. Introduction

The confident foundation of science's vision is of course DNA. Thus the innate specifications for life in its many forms should be found in the specifics of an individual's big DNA molecule. This relationship could - actually should - provide answers to a number of Chapter 1's mysteries, beginning with the amazing abilities of prodigies. This chapter is going to question the veracity of Pinker's (and science's) claim "that life depends on a molecule that carries information, directs metabolism, and replicates itself".

I offer a potentially intuitive introduction to biological inheritance. If you want to see inheritance in a simple direct way then I suggest simply standing in front of a mirror and looking closely at the image. Your basic human physical form represents your gross biological inheritance (as directly derived via DNA from your parents). Additionally, you might be able to see particular facial features that also appear to be derived from one of your parents. In my case I can see such features and they apparently came mostly from my mother. The consistencies between the appearances and form of parents and their offspring certainly seems consistent with the basic biological, DNA-beget, nature dynamic.

Beyond those consistencies there may well be some differences, though, found in your mirror image. Some of the details of a person's facial appearance - including hair styles - may well vary significantly from those of their parents. This, though, should not be surprising and is consistent with a basic environmental/nurture dynamic. Some of those details could be a function of contemporary social trends. Some additional environmental or exposure-based differences may also be apparent. In my case, some accidents left me with scars which have no connection to biological inheritance (and with only a minimal connection to social trends). It seems that our appearances, and perhaps more particularly the appearance of our faces, gives us a simple introduction to biological inheritance and also its partner, environmental influences or experiences. Without dipping into heavy abstractions (and possible contentiousness) one can get a personal sense of the influences of nature and nurture.

The point of this chapter is that many of our innate aspects are not apparent in a mirror, but are important and also presumed to be largely a result of biological inheritance (and thus the common cliche, "its in the genes"). These include our personal behavioral and health tendencies, and the belief in their DNA origins is captured by the corresponding fields, behavioral genetics and personal genomics, respectively. It turns out that these aspects or features are not only significant on a personal level, but they are also presumed to have been key factors in evolution. Additionally, it turns out that the assumption of DNA/genetic origins for such tendencies is increasingly questionable, and it is here that I suggest that science's molecular-only vision is facing general trouble. Furthermore, for those curious about possible big picture support for alternative/religious beliefs, I recommend looking here. If such alternative visions have serious merit then they should challenge materialism is a gross way.

A review of a recent popular book offers another introduction here. A professional reviewer wrote with regards to Siddhartha Mukherjee's 2016 genetics book, *The Gene: An Intimate History* [Mukherjee]:

> [This] is a book we should all read. I shook my head countless times while devouring it, wondering how the author - a brilliant physician, scientist, writer, and Rhodes Scholar could possibly possess so many unique talents. When I closed the book for the final time, I had the answer: must be in the genes [McCarthy].

The Gene is in fact a miserable book, both in its faithful message - "we know [our future is] … in our genes" and in its excessive novelistic style which likely accounted for the very limited endorsement by scientists. With the possible exception of a single paragraph on page 487, at no point does the book hint at the then decade-long, "absolutely beyond belief" failures in genomic searches. In 2019 while reading reviews for *The Gene*, including approximately 500 customer reviews at Amazon, I could not find a single reviewer that bothered to question the loose logic of genetics or comment on the status of DNA searches. To their credit some reviewers did break from the routine adulation of science and criticized the book's writing style [Sludge].

As evident in the response to *The Gene*, there is enormous momentum behind the DNA-based or genetic model of life. It is of course supposed to be a comprehensive "language of life" [Collins]. As a result I suggest that one could easily put together a large book filled with glorious official claims about the workings of DNA. From the broad claims about its presumed role as the basis for the evolution of life down to the many behavioral contributions inferred for human beings (and also other species), DNA has become science's bedrock explanation for life. If the author of such a book could simply obtain a number of endorsements from scientists (preferably big shots) and place them on the back cover, that book could well become a bestseller. And apparently few would question it as suggested in the response to *The Gene*. It is all too easy as an educated person to be bowled over by the certitude surrounding science.

Scientific materialism establishes a foundation for the confidence in DNA. If all of life is simply a function of chemistry then naturally the basis for heredity and the associated biological design must itself come down to molecules. Given the nature of reproduction and some gross connections to DNA (beginning with the male-correlated Y chromosome) there certainly is a basis for starting down the road to what Mukherjee acknowledged is the "religion of genes" [Mukherjee, p.165]. But there are also some serious question marks facing genetic reasoning. One of DNA's accepted roles is to provide "[t]he entire behavioral information available to the newborn" [Mayr, p.253] which is quite astounding in some cases. One such example relates to bird migrations. Some migratory birds have been shown to demonstrate an innate knowledge of their migratory routes and this implies a DNA basis. But is it really plausible for a large molecule - deoxyribonucleic acid (DNA) - to have been shaped by natural selection to encode for the making of a brain equipped with migratory maps or guides? On this point even the Nobel laureate James D. Watson expressed astonishment [Watson 2003].

Temporarily shelving such questions, though, it is helpful to see frank expressions from the underlying materialism. A good example can be found in a May 2017 *Scientific American* article. That article presented recent technical developments designed to observe the dynamics of molecules (involving x-ray based "molecular movies"). In the article the authors, Petra Fromme and John C. H. Spence, offered motivation for their efforts via a quote from the late physicist (and Nobel laureate) Richard Feynman, "Everything that living things do can be understood in terms of the jigglings and wigglings of atoms" [Fromme and Spence]. Those jigglings and wigglings are naturally presumed to follow the predictions of certain equations. Together then life might be seen as a particular subset of the material universe, a subset that could be rather boring to physicists, but is perhaps of more interest to others. Such thinking provides support for materialism and with it the scientifically uncontested claim that "Biology [is] physics" [Mukherjee, p.142].

In fulfilling its blueprint or recipe duties, DNA is supposed to provide the basis for inheritance, which were phenomena that Charles Darwin never understood. The prominent evolutionary biologist Ernst Mayr provided modern biology's answer:

> An understanding of the nature of this variability was finally made possible, after 1900, by advancements in genetics and molecular biology. One can never fully understand the process of evolution unless one has an understanding of the basic facts of inheritance, which explain variation. Therefore the study of genetics [and the encompassing DNA] is an integral part of the study of evolution. But only the heritable part of variation plays a role in evolution [Mayr, p.89].

DNA is thus supposed to provide design codes for organisms and additionally the heritable subset of DNA - the elements that get passed along in conceiving new life - should provide a basis for evolutionary dynamics (along with occasional mutations and environmental changes). Consistent with this role, DNA should also define the innate differences between organisms, both in a gross interspecies sense as well as a more intimate intra-species sense.

A reminder here is that genes consist of subsets of DNA which provide blueprints for the construction of protein molecules in the body. DNA (or the genome) also has significant content beyond the 1.5 percent constituting genes, nevertheless "genes" (and "genetics") tends to be used quite generally. This verbal practice can lead outsiders to think that that is all there is to DNA (or at least its functionality). Regularly this book will go along with this "genetics" tendency. Also along this note on overlap, the term "genotype" can refer to the full sequence of an individual's DNA, or simply their genetic specifics for a condition (such as blood type).

Continuing, a key point for discussions herein is that along with specifying the details of individuals, the genome should thus also specify the innate differences among them. This again is supposed to be true within a species - and thus the field of (human) behavioral genetics - but it is also believed to be critical in a much larger way [Mayr; Croston et al; Hopkins et al]. In this latter sense DNA should specify for the differences in the instinctive behaviors found in different species. Ernst Mayr wrote that:

> There are reasons to believe that behavioral shifts have been involved in most evolutionary innovations, hence the saying "behavior is the pacemaker of evolution." Any behavior that turns out to be of evolutionary significance is likely to be reinforced by the selection of genetic determinants for such behavior (known as the *Baldwin effect*).[Mayr, p.137].

So the behavioral implications associated with a segment of DNA code should be significant to its treatment under natural selection. Therefore a gene that contributes to helpful behavioral inclinations in a species should tend to spread over time, whilst one furthering unhelpful behaviors likely would become less prevalent over time. "Helpful" implying positive contributions to reproductive success. In an artificial modern example, if there was a DNA subset (or a collection of them) in the human collection of DNA codes, that strongly influenced an individual to *not* look both ways before crossing streets, then that particular subset should tend to decline in frequency since bearers thereof would tend to have reduced progeny (as well as lifespans).

Therefore DNA is expected to contribute substantially to the big spectrum of behavioral tendencies found among people (as well as other animals). This is expected to include providing gross explanations for personality differences, including those found between non-monozygotic twin siblings. As an example, if a child stood out in a family in terms of their aggressive inclinations, then the logic of genetics suggests that they are likely to have more aggression-boosting genetic codes than their fellow family members. With this as a backdrop, modern genetics is confidently committed to identifying such genetic origins, including a number of potentially very significant ones. Additionally, beyond some previously identified standout DNA code segments - like the Y chromosome and codes responsible for the increased likelihood of some disease conditions - the ongoing comprehensive genetic searches should greatly fill in our understanding of genetic contributions, and along with this, ourselves. Thus the genomic researcher J. Craig Venter's titled a book *A Life Decoded: My Genome: My Life*.

It turns out that aspects of DNA's expected heritability role can be inferred from human studies. This connection was neatly captured by the psychologist Steven Pinker when he wrote:

> schizophrenia is highly concordant within pairs of identical twins [about 50% of the time when one is affected so is the other twin], who share all of their DNA and most of their environment, but far less concordant within pairs of fraternal twins, who share only half of their [variable] DNA ... and most of their environment. The trick question could be asked - and would have the same answer - for virtually every cognitive and emotional disorder or difference ever observed. Autism, dyslexia, language delay, language impairment, learning disability, left-handedness, major depressions, bipolar illness, obsessive-compulsive disorder, sexual orientation, and many other conditions run in families, are more concordant in identical than in fraternal twins, are better predicted by people's biological relatives than

by their adoptive relatives, and are poorly predicted by any measurable feature of the environment [Pinker 2002, p.46].

So that the many variations in our behavioral inclinations appear to follow biological parent-connected patterns. While variations in innateness are often obvious, its inheritance-packaging is frequently not so obvious (although in terms of physical appearance it certainly can be), but this packaging has become clearer through formal studies. Pinker's statement does, though, appear to shortchange environmental contributions to schizophrenia [Balter].

This type of inheritance relationship also appears to hold in general with disease susceptibilities, thus the medical cliche "it runs in families". In some cases this connection already has an identified DNA-basis, as for example with cystic fibrosis and sickle cell anemia, but much more commonly this relationship is simply assumed. The confidence in that assumption is the basis for the big expectations of the field of personal genomics. Stepping back this inheritance assumption makes straightforward materialist sense, our innate features are supposed to come from our inherited DNA blueprints (except for those associated with a small number of mutations that occurred after conception), which came from our parents. This is both consistent with science's understanding of evolution, and also the similar appearances found between parents and offspring.

But there are some challenges to this logic of inheritance and I will introduce three of them here. First, there are big variations present in identical twins although they share the same DNA specifications. The degree of behavioral consistency or correlation found between identical twins is often only around 50 percent which translates to simply a crude similarity. In the case of male exclusive homosexuality it turns out to only be 20-30 percent [Collins, pp.204-5]. Note that this sexuality characteristic is believed to be in large part binary (expressed or not), unlike personality traits (such as aggressive-versus-passive for example) which appear to be smoothly distributed. These monozygotic differences are a good counterpoint to keep in mind when you encounter remarkable claims about genetic determinism, as for example those inferred via a specific shared behavior found between separately-raised monozygotic twins. James Watson in fact dismissed such examples of apparent determinism as likely being coincidence [Watson 2017, pp.378-9]). Monozygotic twins really are grossly different in a behavioral sense as personal exposure reveals.

A second challenge to genetic logic is that alternative explanations involving environmental influences appear to have quite limited support. Outside of specific fears and a few familial positions (like political affiliation) growing up in a family appears to contribute little to an individual's inclinations [Bouchard et al]. This officially comes across in adoption studies but I suggest that it is also evident in the relatively fixed nature of personality. Together the contributions of these two challenges to DNA logic are succinctly captured in another Pinker quote with regard to behavioral inclinations, "identical twins are 50 percent similar whether they grow up together or apart" [Pinker 2002; p.381]. Thus a basic mystery.

A third and final challenge to the logic of genetics here is an indirect but rather gross one (and perhaps belonged in Chapter 1). That is that behavioral genetics is supposed to reflect the influence of the genome on an individual's brain. Observations of individuals with gross brain deficits raise questions about such reasoning, though. In a 1980 Science article observations by a neurologist John Lorber of a group of patients who were missing large portions of their brains were described [Lewin]. Many of these patients suffered from a condition called hydrocephalus which entails an enlargement of the brain's cerebrospinal fluid reservoirs with consequent losses in the volumes of other brain tissues. That article reported that a number of these patients were left with only about 5 percent of normal brain volume and yet somehow appeared to function normally. Others in this category not surprisingly were severely disabled (and still others with this condition might have died prematurely). Among the normal functioning group Lorber reported that:

> [t]here is a young student at [Sheffield University] who has an IQ of 126, has gained a first-class honors degree in mathematics, and is socially completely normal. And yet the boy has virtually no brain.

Findings like these appear to have been neglected by science and obviously challenge neural and as well as (indirectly) genetic reasoning.

Furthermore, in Lorber's work the symmetry assumption of neuroscience was also challenged. To do this Lorber looked at patients in which the offending ventricle expansion was limited to one side of the brain. Such patients should have seen limitations associated with the compromise of that hemisphere. But as Lorber observed:

> I've now seen more than 50 cases of [such] asymmetrical hydrocephalus and the interesting thing is that only a minority of these individuals show the expected and long-cherished neurological finding of paralysis with spasticity on the opposite side of the body.

He then went on to point out that one of these patients displayed spastic paralysis on the *same* side as their "enormously enlarged ventricles". Why haven't such findings found their way into more neuroscience coverage?

A note for readers here is that in an effort to achieve brevity I have tended to take small relevant excerpts. In the case of Lorber's paper, and a number of other examples, the source is not long, is available online, and is worth a look.

◆ ◆ ◆

Moving along, it turns out that homo sapiens have been referred to by geneticists as a "small species" because there is relatively little genetic variation amongst us and such limited variation is typically found in a species with a small population [Pinker 2002; pp.142-3]. That lack of genetic variation appears to have followed from our having been reduced to a small population not too long ago as we struggled through a difficult period. An insufficient amount of time has since elapsed for our set of DNA variations to expand much (unlike our population). Conveniently, it turns out that any two human beings are about 99.9% identical in terms of their DNA blueprints. This minimal difference translates to being different in only about 3 million bases or letters [Green; Kingsley; Schafer]. In a simple way it is akin to having us all be identical twins, except that there are some notable exceptions beginning with the gender determining (or at least influencing) Y-chromosome.

Of additional note here is that even within the 0.1% variable portion of our genomes, there could be plenty of neutral content (sometimes termed junk) given the haphazard workings of evolution [Zimmer]. A gross way to see this point is to note that some simpler species have much larger genomes than we do. The broad-footed salamander and the onion, for example, have genomes about fifty and five times longer than ours (note this would seem to be a challenge to the logic of intelligent design). A more subtle way to infer the junk/neutral content is implicitly via the soon to be discussed, inability to connect variable DNA to our variable characteristics. Altogether then, among the oft-cited three billion human DNA letters, there is in fact a much smaller subset that is presumed to be home to the origins of our heritable individual distinctions.

Against this evolutionary backdrop the ongoing searches are supposed to identify some specific DNA codes, and hopefully with these identifications, some useful insights into problematic conditions. These searches would then also provide some confirmation of DNA's evolutionary roles. On this point consider the following found in a 2003 *Scientific American* interview with Nobel laureate James D. Watson [Watson 2003]:

> *Scientific American*: [i]n a century, we went from rediscovering Mendel's laws and identifying chromosomes as agents of heredity to having the human genome largely worked out. Finding the double helix drops neatly in the middle of that span. How much, with respect to DNA, is left for us to do? Are there still great discoveries to be made, or is it just filling in details?

And then after some speculation:

> Watson: [relevant research] seems to moving pretty fast. You don't really want to make a guess, but I'd guess that over these next 10 years, the field will be pretty played out. A lot of very good people are working on it. We have the tools. At some stage, the basic principles of genetics will be known be in terms of gene functioning, and then we'll be able to apply that more to [more difficult] problems such as how the brain works.

Scientific American then asked Watson, "[i]f you were starting out as a researcher now". Watson interjected, "I'd be working on something about connections between genes and behavior. You can find genes for behaviors…". His optimism likely reflected the confidence in the DNA model; the limited extent of our variable DNA; and the quality of the then pending research efforts. Given subsequent difficulties encountered in the genetic searches, it is likely that those research efforts have expanded well beyond the expectations in 2003.

◆ ◆ ◆

The big problem facing genetics, though, has been the unfolding inability to find the expected DNA determinants for behavioral as well as disease inclinations. Watson's above-suggested 2013-ish finish line for identifying basic genomic connections was clearly inaccurate. In fact in a 2014 review of another 'breakthrough' in the genetics of intelligence (which purported to account for a possible 1 percent in the variation of innate intelligence), *Scientific American*'s John Horgan pointed out that in a 2012 *Behavioral Genetics* editorial it was pointed out that:

> [t]he literature on candidate gene associations is full of reports that have not stood up to rigorous replication. This is the case both for straightforward main effects and for candidate gene-by-environment interactions...As a result the psychiatric and behavioral genetics literature has become confusing and it now seems likely that many of the published findings of the last decade are wrong or misleading and have not contributed to real advances in knowledge [Horgan].

A significant and under-appreciated story.

The first major acknowledgement came earlier in September 2008, when Duke University's geneticist David Goldstein was quoted with regard to the outcome of thorough (or "tour de force") comparisons between the million or so common genetic variations and the inheritance patterns associated with the occurrences of common complex diseases [Wade 2008]. It was expected that some of these common variations in our DNA blueprints would naturally be correlated with the patterns of susceptibility to common diseases (as well as other heritable characteristics). But Goldstein pointed out that:

> [a]fter doing comprehensive studies for common diseases, we can explain only a few percent of the genetic component of most of these traits. For schizophrenia and bipolar disorder, we get almost nothing; for Type 2 diabetes, 20 variants, but they

explain only 2 to 3 percent of familial clustering, and so on.

Goldstein went on to add:

> It's an astounding thing that we have cracked open the human genome and can look at the entire complement of common genetic variants, and what do we find? Almost nothing. That is absolutely beyond belief.

Note that "common" here implies that a given specific genomic variation is present in at least 5 percent of humans. This initial and very striking result - in particular with regard to the common variants theory in which commonly occurring differences in our DNA were hypothesized to be causally correlated with variations in our complex disease experiences - has been followed by mostly silence amidst subsequent genetic searches.

A simple example of a common variation in DNA is again the Y-chromosome (chromosome denotes a large physically distinct segment of DNA code). About 50% of people have a Y-chromosome in their genome and as a result they have male anatomy. One would similarly expect that some of the other variable code sequences in our DNA would be correlated to other innate differences. Note that such differences do not have to be simple and deterministic (or visible in a mirror), rather they could merely stack the deck in favor of the occurrence of a particular condition. And remember, due to the prevalence of junk or inconsequential DNA sequences, not all of the variations - commonly occurring or otherwise - are expected to have an impact.

This missing heritability (or more tangibly, the missing headline) situation is a huge deal both practically and intellectually. In the above quote Goldstein was assuming that rare genetic variations (variable codes in the DNA which are much less common in their occurrences among people) are responsible for the missing heritability. Yet no substantiated discoveries along those lines, or apparently otherwise, have been reported as of this writing.

The above "beyond belief" quote was reiterated in a subsequent October 2010 *Scientific American* article, "Revolution Postponed" [Hall]. Another frank appraisal also came in 2010 in which Jonathan Latham and Allison Wilson of the Ithaca, New York's Bioscience Resource Project pointed out that with few exceptions (including previously identified genes for cystic fibrosis, sickle cell anemia, and Huntington's disease; and also including genetic contributions for some instances of Alzheimer's and breast cancer):

> according to the best available data, genetic predispositions (i.e. causes) have a negligible role in heart disease, cancer, stroke, autoimmune diseases, obesity, autism, Parkinson's disease, depression, schizophrenia and many other common mental and physical illnesses that are the major killers in Western countries [Latham and Wilson].

They went on to ask (in italics) "[h]ow likely is it that a quantity of genetic variation that could only be called enormous (i.e. more than 90-95% of that for 80 human diseases) is all hiding in what until now [circa 2010] had been considered genetically unlikely places?". Was this point subsequently rebutted by any geneticists? Additionally, Latham and Wilson suggested that "[b]y all rights then, reports of the GWA [genome wide assessments] results should have filled the front pages of every world newspaper for a week".

A subsequent assessment showed up in a May 2017 *Scientific American* article, "Schizophrenia's Unyielding Mysteries: Gene Studies Were Supposed to Reveal the Disorder's Roots. That Didn't Happen. Now Scientists Are Broadening the Search" [Balter]. The author, Michael Balter, described the big DNA search procedure utilized, Genome Wide Assessment Studies (GWAS), as:

scan[ning] the entire genome for differences between the disease and control groups. [They] employ sophisticated statistical analyses to pick up even small increases in the number of specific genetic variants that might contribute to disease risk.

These searches then very carefully check for statistical connections between specific DNA code patterns and the occurrences of supposedly heritably-influenced conditions like schizophrenia. Thus in the jargon of genetics, expecting to identify genotypes (particular codes) contributing to phenotypes (particular outcomes). "Genetic" conditions are of course supposed to reflect actual genetic contributions.

These big schizophrenia genome searches as of 2017 involved a scientific armada numbering over 800 researchers and DNA samples from more than 900,000 subjects. Balter provided a number of superficial positive reports before then offering some realistic ones. In one such assessment David Goldstein, then director of Columbia University's Institute for Genomic Medicine, commented that the C4 finding and the associated possible insight for schizophrenia represents "the first time we have gotten what we wanted out of a GWAS." Additionally, the C4 finding was characterized by one evolutionary genetics researcher, Kenneth Weiss of Pennsylvania State University, in diminutive fashion -" [e]ven if the C4 story is right, it accounts for only a trivial amount of schizophrenia" and that its significance "is debatable".

Another notable assessment in Balter's article came from the behavioral geneticist, Eric Turkheimer, who said that "GWAS shows that schizophrenia is so highly, radically polygenic [i.e., with many DNA contributors] that there may well be nothing to find, just a general unspecifiable genetic background". This seems to be effectively, 'we know that the DNA roots are there (but we just can't find them)'. This conclusion is the opposite of the confidence communicated in *The Gene* or any genetic literature that I am aware of. Finally, David Goldstein provided a critical comment on the nature of the search business in saying that "[p]eople working in the schizophrenia genetics field have greatly over-interpreted their results" and further that they should utilize "a whole lot more humility". How many other areas of the genomic search business are there where this conclusion could apply?

Furthermore, the aforementioned James Watson broke from his earlier optimism and acknowledged the lack of genetic insight into the occurrences of mental illnesses in his 2017 book, *DNA: The Story of the Genetic Revolution*. Watson suggested out that "[t]he history of this research is full of high hopes brought low" [Watson 2017, p.391]. Additionally, he provided a fitting quote on the situation from the geneticists Neil Rich and David Botstein:

> [t]he recent history of genetic linkage studies for [manic depression] is rivaled only by the course of the illness itself. The euphoria of linkage findings being replaced by the dysphoria of non-replication [in other populations] has become a regular pattern, creating a roller coaster-type existence for many psychiatric genetics practitioners as well as interested observers [p.392].

Watson, though, not surprisingly still upheld the faith as reflected when he added that "I am extremely hopeful that we are entering an era of genetic analysis that will soon take us beyond this irritating game of 'now we have it, now we don't'" [p.392].

2. "Dudes, get back to us if and when you have something to report"

A notable genetics research result hit the press in the summer of 2019 and it reflected the outcome of a large study considering the genomic contributions to homosexual behavior. That study and its findings were described in a *New York Times* article, "Many

Genes Influence Same-Sex Sexuality, Not a Single 'Gay Gene'", by Pam Bullock [Bullock]. Additionally, an accompanying article, "What Genetics Is Teaching Us About Sexuality", provided commentary by two researchers, one of whom was involved with the research project [Phelps and Wedow]. Those researchers were biologist Steven M. Phelps of the University of Texas at Austin, and project researcher, sociologist and geneticist Robbee Wedow affiliated with M.I.T and Harvard. Both of these men happen to be gay.

The research described in the two articles might be described as kind of a peak effort by humanistic science. It was a very large and carefully done study and as Bullock's article pointed out, "[e]xperts widely agree that the research was conducted by first-rate scientists" and also it was given a big thumbs up by a relevant researcher at University of Oxford, Melinda Mills, who commented that "if somebody[s] was going to do it, I'm glad they did it". The researchers not only plunged into the relevant scientific analysis, they also labored intensively to put together a sensitive presentation of the findings (nonetheless some researchers even then rejected the study's rationale). Also of note is that trans individuals were not included in the study. As provided in Bullock's article the principal finding from the study, which was based on almost a half a million paired individual behavioral reports and genomes (thus making it the largest of its kind), was that:

> genetics does play a role, responsible for perhaps a third of the influence on whether someone has same-sex sex. The influence comes not from one gene but many, each with a tiny effect - and the rest of the explanation includes social and environmental factors - making it impossible to use genes [alone] to predict someone's sexuality.

By the end of this quote you could feel a little irritated. Likewise, in the article by Phelps and Wedow it is stated that "while biology shapes our most intimate selves, it does so in tandem with our personal histories - with idiosyncratic selves that unfold in larger cultural and social context". Again it seems too loose and awkward.

Nonetheless the study was essentially billed as big genetic success story. But what actually constitutes success? It seems quite ambiguous with its stated conclusion involving many genes "each with a tiny effect". The comments (and for brevity Reader Picks ones) accompanying these articles are somewhat revealing. First, as appears somewhat common, many (probably well-educated) Times' readers seem to simply nod their heads to scientific findings and perhaps second them with everyday expressions like its "[n]ot surprising really" and "[g]enes and environment matter". Also there was a critical theme running through some of the comments to the effect that 'enough with the PC-sensitivities, just give us the facts!'. All of the sensitivity gauntlets that apparently had to be run through before presenting the findings really bothered some readers.

But the real skinny was found in some frank points made in the Reader Picks comments for the Phelps and Wedow article. One of these read:

> [t]his research clearly shows that there is no straight answer - pun unintended. If looking into the DNA of 500,000 people didn't help, what will?

That reader then went on to question efforts to try to understand who we are. Then another reader got a bit animated:

> [l]ess than 1% of variation!
> I almost choked on my pork and beans when I read that. Less than 1% of variation is risible, not even the beginnings of understanding the phenomenon.
> Dudes, get back to us if and when you have something to report.

I appreciated the bluntness (and fun) of this last comment but must now let Bullock's article speak for itself. After going thru generalities the article provided the skinny:

> [r]esearchers specifically identified five genetic variants present in people's genomes that appear to be involved. Those five comprise less that 1 percent of the [inferred] genetic influences, they said.
>
> And when the scientists tried to use genetic markers to predict how people in unrelated data sets reported their sexual behavior, it turned out to be too little genetic information to allow prediction.
>
> 'Because we expect the sum of the effects that we observe will vary as a function of society and over time, it will be basically impossible to predict one's sexual activity or orientation just from genetics," said Andrea Ganna, the study's first author, whose affiliations include the Institute of Molecular Medicine in Finland.

The final bit about varying over time and societal aspects is simply skirting truth. In fact, Mr. "Dudes" accurately pointed out that they really didn't find anything. For additional context, though, Mr. Dudes (officially Dr. Dudes) also asserted a mocking "[h]ello, all behavior is influenced by DNA". To which one might respond "Yes, all behavior is supposed to be shaped or influenced by DNA but that certainly is not what research is revealing". Are there any analogous behavioral genetic studies that have actually identified significant DNA origins? Additionally, exactly what environmental (including "social and cultural") factors have been observed to significantly contribute to this (or other) behavioral tendencies? Finally, how could such factors differentiate the trajectories of monozygotic twin pairs?

One possible reason they didn't find anything is because they chose quite a subtle characteristic to interpret via genetics. The researchers were looking for a DNA connection to those who had answered affirmatively to the question about "whether [one had] ever had sex with a same-sex partner, even once". Is it really realistic to expect a significant genetic connection with this? Likewise, geneticists might expect some kind of DNA contribution for a person being a liberal versus a conservative - but is it also reasonable to expect a DNA connection for crossing over political ideologies in a single case? I suggest that a more meaningful backdrop to this failure here is that they have not already identified significant DNA contributors for those with reversed sexual orientation (i.e., those "born this way"). Such DNA contributions should certainly exist in order to support such transformed orientations (as per genetic logic). In this case, by looking at about a half million behavioral reports and the associated genomes their analysis should likewise have seen corresponding statistical correlation (or blips) reflecting the very high likelihood that individuals with innate homosexual-influencing DNA would have reported same-sex sex. There could be different DNA specifications corresponding to the male and female reverse-sexual orientation contributions, but nonetheless the born-this-way blips should have been there.

Continuing, the article also mentions possible overlap with the genetics of mental illnesses. Somehow the nominal success of their genetic investigation into same-sex sex found overlap with the presumed genetics of mental illnesses. This of course triggered additional sensitive discourse in the article. But it simply highlights the real crisis facing genetics - they can't find significant contributions for many phenomena. The undercurrent of the article relates to its efforts at being sensitive about possible ramifications of their genetic homosexuality findings when in fact the real tension going on - beginning within the researchers themselves - relates to their inability to find anything. These researchers want to find something if only to experience some work satisfaction and also vindicate the basis of their profession.

◆ ◆ ◆

The above same-sex sex study was part of a relatively recent wave of studies which purported to breakthrough and find some significant genetic connections. Earlier in 2018 there were several claiming to find DNA origins for educational attainment and also, indirectly, intelligence. The apparent key to success of these more recent studies was getting data from large numbers of individuals and also some improvements in data processing techniques. As stated in a 2019 *Molecular Psychiatry* article, "Genomic prediction of cognitive traits in childhood and adolescence" [Allegrini *et al*]:

> Progress in predicting cognitive traits from inherited DNA variants has been rapid in the past five years and especially in the past year. Three methodological advances have mainly been responsible for this progress: increasingly large genome-wide association (GWA) studies, genome-wide polygenic scores (GPS) and multivariate analytic tools. The key has been the recognition that the largest associations are extremely small, accounting for less than 0.05% of the [trait] variance. To achieve sufficient power to detect such small sizes, samples in the hundreds of thousands are needed before GWA studies can begin to detect these tiny effects. Because the largest associations are so small, useful predictions of individual differences can only be made by aggregating the effects of thousands of DNA variants in GPS. The third advance is the development of genomic methods that leverage genetic correlations between traits to boost power for variant discovery and polygenic risk prediction.

As is common in reading these reports one has to be leery of their inevitable optimism, but the basic idea is that individual genetic contributions are now being assumed to come in such tiny doses that to detect significant overall genetic import (to say make someone notably more likely to experience a particular condition) it is necessary to look at many people's genomes and trait outcomes, and then to carefully process the big data collection. Additionally, the term "genome-wide" implies using larger samples of an individual's DNA specifics (say than in the earlier mentioned, common variants studies). The resulting processing allows researchers to piece together a large summation formula that can then predict the overall genetic contribution for a particular trait from an individual's DNA specifics. Such a genome-wide polygenic score (or prediction) is supposed to reflect many small contributions of trait-associated genetic variants.

Having not found the expected DNA origins (or at minimum, significant subsets thereof) for many heritable characteristics in earlier studies, many researchers had decided that those origins must be hiding in tiny contributions. This in turn demands very large studies consisting of larger genomic samples. That such big (net) genetic contributions would be hiding amongst so many tiny contributors is striking and seems in contradiction with previously identified single genetic variant-driven conditions. Nonetheless, that is where genetic logic apparently steered much subsequent work.

It is also worth pausing and noting some implications of the hypothesized distributed genetic contributions to contemporary thinking. There recently has been a number of works considering the significance of the presumed coming capability to use genetics to enhance humans. But how likely is that such enhancement is feasible given that it could entail the manipulation of thousands of genetic variants (if they are in fact identified)? In a simple analogy, if someone told you that some desired improvement to your automobile would necessarily require the replacement or modification of hundreds of its parts, would you still consider that work?

Continuing, with regards to one such genome-wide polygenic scores study, a 2018 *Genetics* paper, "Accurate Genomic Prediction of Human Height" [Lello *et al*], claimed a pair of significant findings. Lello *et al* had primarily searched thru the United Kingdom's (UK) Biobank (as did the earlier considered same-sex sex study), and then using almost 500,000 individual data sets they computed genetic predictors including those for height and also educational attainment. In this study the authors appeared to neglect mentioning a likely distinction for the genetic contribution to height. As apparent in the very similar appearances of monozygotic twins, physical attributes like height do seem consistent with genetic logic. The same DNA blueprints are coincident with very similar physical outcomes. Of note here is that this appearance connection could account for a decent chunk of our everyday intuition about genetics. In the case of height the estimated correlation between separated-at-birth monozygotic twins was 0.86 [Bouchard *et al*] (where 1.0 would imply identical heights). Further, a recent estimate for the general heritable contribution to height is 79% (with the remaining 21% of the variance is assumed to somehow come from environmental factors).

Readers can note that in describing variations in traits, this book will often use the everyday term "variation". In reality, though, the statistically-defined entity "variance" is used by researchers as above in characterizing the influences on human height.

The results of Lello *et al*'s study included claims of being able to predict about 40 percent of the variance in individuals' heights. In a more concrete fashion the authors claimed that the "actual heights of most individuals in validation samples are within a few centimeters of the prediction" (which from their graph appears to be roughly plus or minus a couple of inches). From an evolutionary perspective it might be worth noting that given the cumulative nature of height (or length) and also the fact it is a shared attribute among many species, one might reasonably expect that there would be numerous DNA contributions. In fact the authors reported using upwards of about 20,000 genetic variants to form their height predictor. They also felt that their 40 percent success rate was roughly consistent with the limits of their genetic analysis. The authors felt that there is reason to believe that their search pool of DNA variants is still missing out on some significant rare variants (each of which might only show up in a small number of people). In any case, Lello et al exhibited confidence that they were successfully finding the expected DNA origins relevant to determining an individual's height.

The other finding here is Lello *et al*'s genetic predictions for the attribute of educational attainment. Some traits that are simple and routinely recorded like educational attainment are amenable to genetic studies. It is worth noting that such traits can be quite loose in their implications, though. A very wide range in educational achievement can be associated with the nominal attainment of being a high school graduate. Nonetheless, Lello *et al* reported identifying a genetic basis for educational attainment and it appeared to predict about 9 percent of its variability. A number of other large concurrent studies also targeted educational attainment and with it indirectly, intelligence (including [Lee *et al*; Allegrini *et al*; Plomin and Stumm]). Due to rough correlations between educational attainment (and a few other commonly recorded attributes) and intelligence, you can take a stab at estimating IQs using other measures.

What I would suggest here, though, is that the polygenic findings associated with height prediction could be qualitatively different from the cognitive predictions. When people use thousands of variants to come up with roughly a 40 percent explanation for the variation in height, that should probably be taken more seriously than analogous efforts to obtain 10 percent or so of the variation in educational attainment (and with it intelligence). These large efforts involving many small contributors are fraught with possible errors and thus perhaps 10 percent is still in the shadow of errors or statistical noise.

In fact, one possible error source in these large polygenic studies is population stratification. Human beings of course are somewhat aligned into separate groups. Such groups really do have their own particular DNA variants or markers which is how DNA-based individual histories can be created at companies like ancestry<dot>com. Where this can present a challenge, though, is when genetic researchers are trying to differentiate people based on their genetic propensities. They obviously do not want to declare simple genetic markers based on group history to be significant to a trait when they are not. One simple example I have seen given in the literature is with regards to the ability to eat with chop sticks. Naively researchers attempting to uncover some genetic determinants for such facility could inadvertently uncover genetic markers for having East Asian ancestry. The general point here is that groups really can differ in their trait characteristics independently of any underlying genetic basis (this can of course also be significant to a trait like education attainment). It turns out to be quite tricky to normalize genetic search results by possible interference from this population stratification phenomenon [Young].

Continuing with the consideration of polygenic scores, it turned out that in 2019 complications with these studies were encountered. Some earlier studies attempted to uncover the evolutionary genetic dynamics underlying the fact that southern Europeans tend to be shorter than northern Europeans. Some initial analyses were positive in that genetic contributors were apparently uncovered. Two later works, though, in applying those findings to the larger and more homogenous UK Biobank data set did not corroborate this [Berg *et al*; Sohail *et al*]. The new data set (which obviously still involved adults of various heights) produced somewhat different estimates for the small contributions of genetic variants that had been found in the earlier study. When subsequently run through the polygenic score algorithm those adjusted variant scores produced overall height predictions that contradicted the earlier studies' claimed genetic basis for southern Europe's shorter populations. Note that this focused look at genetic contributions to height (among Europeans) might in fact raise doubts over the earlier general 40 percent claim (and also my suggested support for it).

Based on the two contradictory study findings a 2019 *Genomics* article, "New Turmoil Predicting the Effects of Genes" was produced [Cepelewicz]. That article's conclusions strongly suggested that the polygenic successes thus far had been unknowingly tainted by complications including population stratification. One researcher, Nick Barton of the Institute of Science and Technology Austria, said:

> [t]he whole thing is tricky, because the origins of genetic variation in any population are really complicated. Now you really can't take at face value any of these methods over the last four or five years that use polygenic scores.

Another researcher, Shamil Sunyaev of Harvard Medical School, commented that "no one realized how big of a problem" the population phenomena was. An additional researcher commented that "[i]t's fairly humbling to see all of that work go away".

One early warning sign with regards to the polygenic accuracy was that their prediction performances showed group dependency. In fact, for a group of African Americans considered, their educational attainment predictor failed. Some of the early reports tended to rationalize such group differences as making environmental sense, but that seems doubtful. Should variations in cognitive characteristics (or height) really have genetic origins which are group-dependent?

In reviewing thru the polygenic score landscape I encountered the work of a retired psychiatrist, Steve Pittelli [Pittelli 2020] and [Pittelli 2018]. Pittelli had apparently been following the genetic revolution from the psychiatry neighborhood for a number of years. He claims to have spent these years observing what I tend to think of as the cycle of genetic breakthroughs. One publicized breakthrough followed by another, with little mention of their contradictions and discontinuities. Significantly, this cycle offers a superficial ongoing veneer of success for genetics. In the world of psychiatry Pittelli observed that the promise of genetics was largely and uncritically accepted and this markedly displaced other approaches in the field. Pittelli in a nicely written essay in *Logos* - nominally focused on reviewing Robert Plomin's book *Blueprint: How DNA Makes Us Who We Are* - Pittelli covered a sizable swath of the contemporary genetics efforts and its under-appreciated dangers. His coverage is not akin to the somewhat routine efforts to brace against genetic determinism (i.e., 'it is not all in the genes!') which even geneticists now embrace. Pittelli bothered to follow the cycle of contradictory breakthroughs to their likely conclusion, DNA is striking out as a cognitive prediction vehicle in a big way, in particular in the area of mental health.

3. Some Additional Context and Possible Explanations

For more context on the missing heritability problem, you can look to Ernst Mayr's *What Evolution Is* which provides an excellent synopsis of science's understanding of evolution [Mayr]. Mayr's book highlights two scientific assumptions about evolution. The first is that evolutionary processes simply reflect physics-dictated phenomena, with no underlying direction. Molecules just doing their thing. Mayr not surprisingly offers little defense of this physics-only assumption. The second assumption is that DNA is capable of fulfilling its life/evolutionary roles and Mayr doesn't even acknowledge this assumption. As science sees it, all of life must be material-only and thus consistent with physics. This confidence in materialism-only evolution is nicely captured in Mayr's book, beginning with its title.

That complete confidence in DNA's functioning is also reflected in the earlier mentioned 2016 book, *The Gene*, by Siddartha Mukherjee and unfortunately largely echoed in its reception. Mukherjee's book captured the materialist nature of genetics and thus life. Although he in a surprisingly common contradiction also tries to undo the determinism of DNA (see for example his discussions on intelligence). It is also noteworthy that Mukherjee made a point of predicting success for the genomic searches by "the end of the decade". As of this writing in 2024 is that prediction looking accurate? An earlier look at the early 2019 Amazon reviews for *The Gene* reveals almost all 5 star reviews, with one 3 star review apparently protesting the lack of political correctness in a politically correct-oriented book! One of the 5 star reviews really captured the modern tendency towards science-bent rapture, "[a] Majestic and brilliant work, beautifully written, and informative, and evocative". A subsequent look at reviews in 2022 revealed mostly five star reviews with a few low scores reflecting critical takes on the book's simplistic presentation. Similarly, is James D. Watson's "extremely hopeful" take on genetics and mental illnesses panning out? As of this writing I have seen nothing consistent with significant success in either behavioral genetics or personal genomics.

At this point I think that it looks likely that behavioral genetics and personal genomics will fall grossly short of their expectations. If the missing heritability situation reflected an "absolutely beyond belief" failure in 2008, then it has to be a notch up in 2024. Furthermore, the unsuccessful status of the genetic searches also argues for plenty of non-functional content among the variable portions of our genomes. If you compare the outcomes of many individuals differing in one or more variable DNA-lettering and find no corresponding differences in their outcomes, then that suggests those variable codes could well have little functional significance. This appears in line with existing claims about the prevalence of junk or neutral DNA. One evolutionary biologist, T. Ryan Gregory, has claimed that given the haphazard dynamics of evolution that "only 8 percent, plus or minus 1 percent" of human DNA is likely to be functional [Zimmer].

On this point it is noteworthy that intelligent design work (see for example *Darwin's Doubt* by Stephen C. Meyer) appears to imply that there is minimal junk content in DNA. This might make sense from the perspective of the intelligent designer hypothesis but with the additional evidence that even our variable DNA contains plenty of non-functional elements, that design hypothesis is undermined.

So if the origins of our individual behavioral inclinations turn out to be independent of our DNA, then how much confidence should we have in a genetic basis for the gender- or species-specific behavioral tendencies that are presumed by evolutionary psychology? Differences in innate behavioral aspects are supposed to have their roots in DNA differences, whether they happen to occur between two same-sex individuals or more broadly between the standard equipment of different genders and/or species.

◆ ◆ ◆

Continuing it is worth looking at two possible alternative explanations for the missing heritability. One explanation was given in a 2010 article that was previously quoted. That was the interesting and significant "The Great DNA Deficit: Are Genes for Disease a Mirage" article by Jonathan Latham and Allison Wilson of Ithaca, New York's Bioscience Resource Project. In that article they laid out what they feel is a strong case against the existence of the DNA origins expected in personal genomics.

Their claim is that the origins of complex disease occurrences are simply environmental, and that the apparent heredity reflects faulty studies involving the relative outcomes of monozygotic (identical) and dizygotic (fraternal) twin pairs. Latham and Wilson appeared to build their environmental argument by first looking at accepted environmental causes.

They pointed out that "[p]eople who migrate acquire the spectrum of diseases of their adopted country". Their citation here was to the results described in *The China Study* by Cornell University's T. Colin Campbell along with his son, Thomas M. Campbell II [Campbell]. That study appeared to demonstrate strong statistical correlations between our diet and the likelihood of our encountering common complex diseases, which include cancer and heart disease (the strength of the study was that up until not too long ago many people in China lived local lives and consumed the corresponding traditional local diets, and ultimately exhibited disease occurrence rates seemingly correlated with location). The resulting recommendation was to move towards a whole foods, plant-based diet. The overlapping Ithaca origins of that popular study and the Bioscience Resource Project could account for a decent chunk of Latham and Wilson's commitment to an environmental explanation.

As it turns out I am a fan of *The China Study* and also vegan, but I don't accept Latham and Wilson's reasoning here. The recommended plant-based diet may be helpful health-(and also sustainability-)wise, but that does not preclude the possibility of significant innate factors being also at work. Such factors might then differentiate the outcomes of individuals who happen to eat similar diets and also have similar environmental exposures. Such innate factors scientifically are supposed to have DNA origins (as they certainly do for established genetic conditions). Geneticists have been doing twin studies for a long time now and they have consistently demonstrated that monozygotic twins pairs tend to be more consistent in their disease experiences than are fraternal twin pairs. This relationship has been observed across a variety of disease conditions. Such studies suggest for example that about 80 percent of the cause of the occurrence of the mental illness schizophrenia is genetic [Balter] and the remaining 20 percent is environmental. That high estimate reflects that there is a roughly 50 percent concurrence rate amongst monozygotic twin pairs versus only about 10 percent amongst dizygotic (or fraternal) pairs. Thus, if you are a monozygotic twin and your twin sibling experiences schizophrenia then it is appears to be about 50 percent likely that you will too.

There certainly are very significant environmental connections for diseases as for example found between smoking and lung cancer. But there also is long established evidence of differing innate susceptibility factors across a number of diseases for individuals and also as grossly evident in the patterns of disease occurrences among families. Does it seem reasonable to think that the susceptibility to schizophrenia and autism can be tied completely to diet and/or other environmental factors? Additionally, beyond experiencing trauma, can they suggest environmental factors contributing to either of these conditions? The occurrence rates for schizophrenia appear to be "about 1 percent throughout the world, notwithstanding vast environmental and socioeconomic differences across societies" [Balter]. Latham and Wilson bring in some arguments from the earlier Nature versus Nurture academic battles, arguments in particular that appear to write off twin studies due to purportedly flawed assumptions and even going so far as to cite an academic's claim that "human heritability ... [is] a 'poisonous concept'". I think that the straightforward logic used to estimate heritability using twins makes sound scientific sense.

Instead of going into elaborate arguments with regards to environmental versus innate contributions, I think it is probably better to walk away from the subtle disease susceptibility realm (can you look at person you meet and sense such susceptibilities?). Looking in the behavioral inclination arena, on the other hand, offers much clearer evidence for the variable aspect of innate characteristics. Is any non-academic-affiliated adult willing to argue that there aren't clear innate differences in personalities and also in gross behavioral phenomena? This should be readily apparent to anyone who grew up with siblings. These differences show up early and appear to be rather deeply etched and thus are presumed to have genetic bases. Notice also that even if these tendencies were caused by spontaneous mutations (as opposed to passed along directly from parents), then some of the mutation's genetic details should still show up in DNA searches. Furthermore, for those wanting a vivid sample of the variations in human intelligence, let me suggest doing some volunteer tutoring. Analogous to sports, you will likely encounter big differences in capacities. There may be other forms of intelligence as some have argued, but there certainly is evident a conceptual learning attribute termed "intelligence" and, for better and not better, it is rather significant in the modern world.

Latham and Wilson went further down a questionable track in that they introduced politicians and corporations. Both of these entities are claimed to "like genetic determinism" because it can shift blame for ill-health in the public away from them.

◆ ◆ ◆

Continuing here with a second possible heredity explanation, I consider Rupert Sheldrake's extension of existing ideas involving morphogenetic fields. Sheldrake builds on earlier efforts which argued against the plausibility of DNA being able to fully specify our innate details. In particular, how is it that DNA - which codes for the linear layout of amino acids comprising proteins - can ultimately specify our very complicated forms? In addition to the big coverage in his book, *The Presence of the Past* [Sheldrake 2012a], Sheldrake also offers more succinct descriptions including a one page synopsis [Sheldrake bet]. That page is paired with the biologist Lewis Wolpert's contrary synopsis and together they form a modest bet. In Sheldrake's one page statement he begins with a sort of bottom-up argument against the plausibility of genetics:

> [g]enes code for the linear sequences of amino acids in proteins, which then fold up into complex three-dimensional forms. Wolpert's wager presupposes that the folding of proteins can be computed from first principles, given the sequence of amino acids

specified by the genes. So far, this has proven impossible. As in all bottom-up calculations, there is a combinatorial explosion. For example, by random folding, the amino acid chain of the enzyme ribonuclease, a small protein, could adopt more than 10^{40} different shapes, which could take billions of years to explore. In fact, it folds into its habitual form in 2 minutes.

The folding of proteins does appear to be a big complexity challenge, but I think that it is likely that many of the claimed 10^{40} different shapes are not possible. A linear sequence cannot be folded in such a way as to produce overlapping positioning of different atoms. Additionally, Sheldrake also furthered his implausibility case by suggesting that the complexity challenges for establishing the structure of cells are even worse. He went on to introduce the hypothesized approach based on fields:

> [r]andom molecular permutations simply cannot explain how organisms work. Instead, cells, tissues and organs develop in a modular manner, shaped by morphogenetic fields, first recognized [or hypothesized] by developmental biologists in the 1920s.

The idea here is that physical fields somehow channel the developing embryo towards an endpoint of an organism's physical form (and also more subtly, the corresponding behavioral patterns). In this way DNA is claimed to simply provide molecular recipes for the body's proteins, while morphogenetic fields are claimed to shape those ingredients into functioning organisms.

(A subtle aside here. Starting about a year ago there were reports of using pattern recognition - nominally Artificial Intelligence - to make headway on this problem. If that is true and ultimately beneficial then that is good news. The subtle part, though, is that recognizing patterns is not the same as physically explaining or modeling the phenomenon. Perhaps such pattern recognition could also find connections between the weather experienced in two far away locations. But that does not constitute a physical explanation. Thus Sheldrake's hypothesis with regard to the folding problem would appear to stand as plausible.)

Rupert Sheldrake appears convinced that the original ideas involving fields are roughly accurate. A contribution of his appears to be hypothesizing that such fields are a memory-bearing aspect of reality. In *The Presence of the Past* he suggested [Sheldrake 2012a, pp.154-5]:

> developing organisms are tuned to similar past organisms, which act as morphic "transmitters". Their tuning depends on the presence of appropriate genes and proteins, and genetic inheritance helps explain why they are tuned in to morphic fields of their own species: a frog's egg tunes in to frog fields rather than newt or goldfish fields because it is already a frog cell containing frog genes and proteins.

And thus "the forms of the cells, tissues, organs, and the organisms as a whole are shaped not by DNA but by morphic fields". Furthermore, Sheldrake suggested that:

> inherited behavior of animals is likewise organized by morphic fields. Genetic changes can affect both the form and behavior, but these patterns of activity are inherited by morphic resonance.

In a very broad way Sheldrake feels that a number of mysteries in life - beginning with inheritance - imply the existence of a series of shaping or guiding fields.

I find Sheldrake's works to be very interesting (and he certainly covers a lot of ground), although they can sometimes be a bit of a challenge for me personally because of their philosophical style. He included a significant point with regard to the implications of proposed intelligent design-based ideas. In *The Presence of the Past*, he pointed out that such theories really don't challenge materialism (and with it the associated determinism), there would just imply some external intelligent input into ongoing evolutionary processes. In the end, though, there would still be molecules acting like molecules and that paradigm would define life as we know it. I agree about on the lack of significance of such design proposals. But how does the introduction of a whole bunch of information or morphic fields change life, or more particularly, who/what we are? It seems to be just more physics inserted along with the existing ingredients and in the end life could still be defined via physical processes (albeit now more complicated), resulting in the same basic implications that entities like self and free will are just artifacts (or emergent phenomena) which are derived from physics (and thus equations).

This contradiction is significant in that Sheldrake's work appears to be motivated not just to challenge the existing scientific vision, but also support a deeper vision of life. For example he wrote, "[t]he Father is the source of the formative principle" [Sheldrake 2012a, p.357] and "[f]rom the very beginning, the universe has been inflated as if by a creative breath blowing it up" [p.357]. He has also written 3 books on spirituality - *Science and Spiritual Practices: Transformative Experiences and Their Effects on Our Bodies, Brains, and Health*; *Ways to Go Beyond and Why They Work: Spiritual Practices in a Scientific Age*; and *The Physics of Angels: Exploring the Realm Where Science and Spirit Meet*. But if morphic fields are simply physical fields - presumably then ultimately following some equations - then how does that change the deterministic implications of materialism?

On the other hand, given the unfolding crisis confronting the genetics, Sheldrake should not be shunned or ridiculed by biologists. His heresy does not appear to be serious like any form of dualism would be, it simply appears to entail more elaborate and novel physics (including the presence of memory within the morphic fields). Continuing, in *The Presence of the Past* Sheldrake seems to claim that these morphic ideas could also be extended into useful explanations of our "evolving" universe. He also refers to "evolutionary cosmology" as though it were an established entity. I have not been able to find references consistent with this evolutionary assertion, though. Perhaps he went a bit overboard in trying to generalize the morphic concept.

More critically, though, I think that Sheldrake's heredity explanation seems anchored in an inaccuracy. He went to considerable lengths to suggest that the incredible similarities noted amongst monozygotic twins, in particular those who were raised separately, were not simply the result of genes. He wrote:

> morphic resonance between [monozygotic twins] will be exceptionally specific and stronger than that between any other pairs of humans. As a result, patterns of activity, beliefs, habits, or health patterns in one are likely to influence the other. Therefore, many of the remarkable similarities between identical twins may depend on morphic resonance rather than genes [Sheldrake 2012b, p.182].

The idea here is that physical fields are likely needed to explain some of the amazing similarities such as when separated shortly after birth identical twins have been found to both live in "the only house on the block, with a white bench around a tree in the backyard; both were interested in stock car racing; both had elaborate workshops where they made miniature picnic tables or miniature rocking chairs" [Sheldrake 2012b, p.180].

Steven Pinker similarly claimed that despite gross differences in environmental exposures:

> [i]dentical twins separated at birth share traits like entering the water backwards and only up to their knees, sitting out elections because they feel insufficiently informed, obsessively counting everything in sight, becoming captain of the

volunteer fire department, and leaving little love notes around the house for their wives [Pinker 1997, p.20].

An earlier mentioned alternative explanation, though, was provided by the biologist James D. Watson. In it such shared behaviors likely reflect coincidences [Watson 2017, pp.378-9]. Watson offered an example in that he and his two (unrelated) coauthors had all owned Volvo station wagons.

The important point missing here, though, is that the big mystery posed by monozygotic twins is not their similarities, but the scale of their differences. The fact that their appearances are typically so similar makes sense genetically (possibly furthered by something akin to morphogenetic resonance). The fact that they are wholesale different in a behavioral sense does not, and thus the same Steven Pinker concluded that "something is happening here but we don't know what it is" [Pinker 2002, p.380]. This is a well established mystery in psychology and this should have tempered Pinker et al's endorsement of genetic determinism. Moreover this finding is readily apparent in person. In an effort to try to make sense of this mystery the researcher Judith R. Harris wrote the book *No Two Alike*. That book appropriately opens with one identical twin telling a reporter that she and her twin "have different world views, we have different lifestyles, we think very differently about issues" [Harris J. R., p.1]. Additionally, the twin added "[w]e are two completely separate individuals who are stuck to each other". Those twins were conjoined and sadly died as a result of their separation surgery. But are such differences really surprising given the differences observable between other monozygotic twins, whether they were raised together or apart? How this can happen given the assumptions of genetics (and materialism) is a serious question. How this can happen when morphic fields are supposed to make them more similar should make Sheldrake curious.

Furthermore, if we are to take nurture/environmental explanations seriously, like those suggested by Latham and

Wilson, then how can such differences show up between monozygotic twins regardless of whether they grew up together or not? The significant health differences observed between monozygotic twins were described in a 2006 *New York Times* article by Gina Kolata [Kolata]. Kolata's article began by describing an active and healthy 92 year old and also her monozygotic twin. They had both grown up together and went on to live in the same area. The other twin, though, had had a hip replaced; had experienced incontinence; had experienced a "degenerative disorder that destroyed most of her vision"; and she also had dementia. Describing those differences was an appropriate warmup to the rest of the article which discussed the very surprising differences observed in a large study on twin longevity. Monozygotic/identical twins' longevities turned out to be only a little closer than those of dizygotic/fraternal twins, and the monozygotic twins were found to die on average "more than 10 years apart". Going further with this, one of the study's authors commented that "how tall your parents are compared to the average height explains 80 to 90 percent of how tall you are compared to the average person [but] only 3 percent of how long you live compared to the average person can be explained by how long your parents lived". Results like this should have received more attention and should have moderated science's genetic expectations as well as those for environmental-based ideas.

4. Some Perspective from Physics and Psychiatry

For some context here a comparison with physics' really big topic of dark matter. From careful astronomical observations it is apparent that the visible matter of the universe provides an inadequate basis for the large scale motions of the universe. Somehow there are some additional forces at play. Two kinds of these forces are hypothesized. One is an attractive or gravity-like force and it is presumed to arise from non-visible stuff termed "dark matter". Somehow then this invisible dark matter results in gravity-like forces which are believed to be responsible for the unaccounted for attractive forces implicit in the motions within galaxies. The other mysterious force is thought to be responsible for the accelerating expansion of the universe and it is termed "dark energy". This is currently hypothesized to be a property of space and it is somehow causing the unaccounted for acceleration of galaxies spreading apart. These two together, in a gravity (and thus mass-like) sense for dark matter, and in an energy-based sense for dark energy, are thought to makeup something like 95% of the mass-energy of the universe. Thus "normal" matter - the stuff we can directly observe and physics has historically examined - constitutes a small piece of the universe.

In the case of the mystery of dark matter, there have been big research efforts underway for three decades now to try to detect the hypothesized dark particles. Researchers in particular have been looking for signs of interaction between dark matter particles and regular matter (in a terrestrial setting). In a *Scientific American* article, "Is Dark Matter Real?", by Sabin Hossenfelder and Stacy S. McGaugh [Hossenfelder and McGaugh] these efforts were described as experiments that:

> place large tanks of liquified noble gases or carefully prepared solids, kept at extremely low temperatures, in well-shielded environments such as underground mines to avoid contamination from cosmic radiation. Sensitive detectors patiently wait for telltale signs of a dark matter particle bouncing off an atomic nucleus in the liquid or solid target.

Hossenfelder and McGaugh then went on to point out that none of these searches has uncovered evidence for dark particles. Additionally, the authors also point out some challenges for any explanation involving dark matter. Conceptually while such invisible particles could provide some of the missing gravity necessary to explain the motion within galaxies, they appear challenged in trying to explain some more subtle aspects of galactic dynamics.

Hossenfelder and McGaugh then went on to discuss a potential alternative take on the mystery. That alternative is that what astronomers have been seeing is in fact a result of some novel aspects of the force of gravity. They refer to these potential explanations as "modified gravity" theories. This is inherently a bit heretical since the approach requires questioning the completeness of Einstein's theory of general relativity. It also doesn't require additional particles. The authors do what appears to be a good job of providing balanced arguments, for and against, this alternative explanation involving a modified form of gravity.

What is of significance here with regards to the missing heritability situation is that in the missing dark matter scenario, physicists have a plan B to consider. Although the pursuit of plan B runs into substantial inertia - due to its challenging of Einstein's theory and also the particle-searching inclinations of physicists - researchers can consider plan B and apparently keep their jobs and even get published in *Scientific American*. Hossenfelder and McGaugh pointed out in their 2018 article that currently "a few dozen of scientists are studying modified gravity, whereas several thousand are looking for particle dark matter". The plan B research effort then might still be chugging along in modest fashion.

On the other hand, with the heritability deficit I suggest there is little analogous freedom for geneticists. The fixed scientific belief that life is completely describable in terms of physics dictates that DNA fulfill the heredity role (and thus be the language of life). For a sense of the situation a couple of quotes from James D. Watson will do:

> I was born curious. ... And so if you wanted an explanation for life, it had to be about the molecular basis for life. I never thought there was a spiritual

basis for life; I was very lucky to be brought up by a father who had no religious beliefs [Watson 2003].

And with regard to a promotional line used for the genetics-inspired movie *Gattaca* - "There is no gene for the human spirit" - Watson wrote, "[i]t remains a dangerous blind spot in our society that so many wish this were so" [Watson 2017, p.440]. Readers might keep Watson's scientific perspective and potential blind spot in mind.

There is one conceivable alternative materialist basis for some heredity, though, and that is in the form of epigenetic contributions. Epigenetics involves information stored not directly in the DNA letter sequence, but instead in the form of the physical packaging of the long string-like DNA molecule. Such packaging can indirectly regulate the expression (or replication) of genes by for example hiding or embedding particular genetic sequences. If one visualizes a genome as an extremely long ladder in which sequences of steps encode for different proteins, then one might extend that visual aid to include the possibility that through epigenetic mechanisms some substantial knots can be formed in the huge ladder. Such knots in turn can influence the protein replication process.

Established functional aspects of epigenetics consist of its allowing for the specialization of cells for different tissues, and also in some apparent contributions towards the conditioning of the brain. The latter process has been considered as another possible route for inheritance. But it appears that even epigenetic researchers are very modest with their expectations in this regard. One particular area in which experimental evidence has been suggestive of extra-genetic contributions to heredity, is in the context of psychological trauma [Carey]. In an overview of possible epigenetic heredity contributions, the researcher Eric Nestler claimed that "[o]f course we now know that an individual's genes play the dominant [heredity] role in determining physiology and function" [Nestler]. Nestler went on in a follow-up conversation to state that any epigenetic inheritance effect is "controversial" [Nestler podcast]. That controversy reflects the apparent obstacles to any inheritance via epigenetic mechanisms. Those obstacles are formidable and thus many geneticists completely reject that possibility [Carey]. Consistent with this James Watson described those epigenetic-heredity hurdles [Watson 2017, p.384]. In brief, the molecules contributing to the epigenetic-packaging (or shaping) of the genome are believed to be stripped off twice before forming egg and sperm cells (and thus in the above ladder analogy any epigenetic knots would be undone). Thus Watson claimed, "the DNA that goes into the eggs and sperm are stripped clean of epigenetic marks [or molecules], resulting in the fertilized egg being the epigenetic equivalent of a blank slate".

One possible opening for epigenetic contributions to inheritance, though, was pointed out by the epigenetic epidemiologist, Karin Michels. Michels suggested that could happen:

> through a distinct and poorly understood mechanism called genomic imprinting. This transgenerational inheritance seems to be limited to genes that control growth during fetal development [Shaw].

In that nice succinct article, Michels also made clear how difficult it is to weed out possible effects in offspring that were truly inherited (including from epigenetic sources) from those based on environmental exposures in the womb. This difficulty she believed casts a significant doubt on a number of the claims involving epigenetic inheritance. In conclusion it appears that there could be a small window for some epigenetic inheritance. A related mystery would then seem to be how such epigenetic marks would then migrate through the developmental stages, and on to their previous cell type where they could then echo the effects found in their parents (likely in some type of brain cell for behavioral impacts).

One might simply keep prodigal behaviors in the back of your mind when contemplating challenges facing any form of bio-chemical inheritance mechanism. It isn't the proverbial Rocket Science to realize that there are things that appear implausible from the materialist perspective.

◆ ◆ ◆

For some personal perspectives on the genetics landscape, one can read Andrew Solomon's engaging big book about unusual children and their families, *Far From the Tree* [Solomon 2012]. When reading Solomon's book it is easy to be impressed with the mysteries some of the children represent. It is also very easy to be moved by the parental challenges those children represent and also by the corresponding parental commitments they can elicit. Solomon did not have a scientist's background so his discussions about these situations tend to range far and wide (and perhaps include too much psychoanalytical speculation). On the other hand, possible genetic explanations regularly show up in *Far From the Tree*. In addition to conditions involving previously identified mutations like Down's Syndrome (involving the presence of an extra copy of chromosome 21), the remaining unusual innate conditions considered in Solomon's book are also expected to have some genetic origins. In his chapter on kids who grew up to commit crimes and moreover seemed criminally inclined, Solomon wrote that [Solomon 2012, p.563-4]:

> [a]rguments about the nature-or-nurture origin of criminality are just as engaged as those about the origin of autism or genius. The National Institutes of Health's Maribeth Champoux and her colleagues have shown that newborn monkeys with a gene for extreme aggression will not grow up to be aggressive if they are cross-fostered to extremely gentle mothers, even though the aggression gene is still biologically

active in them. In human beings, criminal behavior has been related to a genetic irregularity associated with changed function in a particular serotonin transporter.

Solomon also pointed out that in humans, "the [aggression] gene appears to confer not criminal behavior, but a vulnerability to develop such behavior under certain circumstances". Here we see a belief in a genetic contribution as well as the rather common tendency to weaken possible genetic determinism.

What is of significance here is that these confident discussions published in 2012 are now forgotten. Like many other genetic findings they were perhaps initially marginal and since have been negated. Readers can look up discussions in a book like Pinker's *Better Angels of Our Nature* for some established rebuttals to such aggression gene findings (but naturally paired with arguments ultimately supporting some genetic basis) [Pinker 2011, pp.611-22]. In this way the missing heritability problem is perhaps most tangible as the missing headline problem. If science truly had a solid handle on an aggression gene(s) it would have been huge news. In a publication like the *New York Times* it would have produced a very big front page headlines and stories. Furthermore the *Times* would have certainly had additional articles to allay fears about genetic determinism, perhaps in the form of articles describing people that had made notable positive contributions despite possessing the dreaded aggression-promoting gene(s). Furthermore, significant findings of other DNA connections would have certainly produced large media follow-up.

Other aspects of genetic reasoning were also touched on in *Far From the Tree*. In a chapter on raising children who were conceived as a result of rape, Solomon presented a number of poignant examples. In one of those genetic reasoning showed up in a mom's quote:

[h]alf of her genes are evil ... I can do whatever I should as her mom to make her this loving, wonderful, caring person. But in her is the DNA of a person who is really sick, and is that DNA stronger than what I can do? [Solomon 2012, p.484].

Such genetic reasoning is a natural fallout from the modern understanding of life, in effect a vision which Sam Harris characterized as being consistent with life as consisting of biochemical puppets. Further genetic import can be found in the enormous financial and intellectual commitment to uncovering the expected DNA origins. There really is a lot on the line with the missing heritability situation.

Of additional note here was a 2022 New York Times article, "The 'Nation's Psychiatrist' Takes Stock, With Frustration" by Ellen Barry [Barry]. That article reflected on a then new book by the retired head of the National Institute of Mental Health, Dr. Thomas P. Insel, who had headed NIMH for 13 years. During that period he had helped NIMH steer their resources "away from behavioral research and toward neuroscience and genetics [or a basic science approach]". Insel as he put it, "bet big on genomics." One of his book's conclusion was that ever bigger searches were required implying that many variants making even "smaller and smaller effects" were somehow responsible. Insel - like other geneticists - essentially had to draw this conclusion. He in fact stated that we need to "double down" on basic research. His successor, Joshua A. Gordon also commented on the need to continue down this genetic road but also acknowledged that genetic treatments for the conditions of autism, schizophrenia, and bipolar disorder were "not likely to pan out in the next five or 10 years". Perhaps instead of speaking/writing essentially on auto-pilot, they should be considering that their assumption is wrong.

Natural science's materialist fixation also came out indirectly in interview with an early opponent of the genomic approach, Dr. Allen Frances of Duke University, who recently said:

[t]he end result of these last 30 years is an exciting intellectual adventure, one of the more fascinating pieces of science in our lifetimes, but it hasn't helped a single patient.

Even a critic felt compelled to put a positive spin on what has been an enormous failure (for details on the vast scope of the efforts and their outcome see the aforementioned "Schizophrenia's Unyielding Mystery" [Balter]). Author Ellen Barry wrote with regard to the mental health crisis in America it:

[c]alls out a paradox: that the United States, a country that leads the world in spending on medical research, also stands out for its dismal outcomes in people with mental illnesses. Indeed, over the last three decades, even as government invested billions of dollars in better understanding the brain, by some measures the outcomes have deteriorated.

The article then quoted Insel in an optimistic take on the crisis in that it is "not a research problem, it's an implementation problem ... [g]ood treatments for serious diseases like schizophrenia and bipolar disorder already exists". Really?

I add a local note on this situation. I live very close to an abandoned psychiatric facility, Rochester's State Mental Hospital or simply Terrence Tower. There is fine online video ("Echo of the Past: The Terrence Tower") chronicling people's experiences there which often were very unpleasant. I see that 16 floor tower as constituting a monument to the hubris of science. Its original (and likely confident) mission was to cure those with mental illnesses.

The neglected and significant mystery is that "[s]chizophrenia has a more benign course and outcome in the developing world" [Luhrmann 2012]. In fact in our country people with schizophrenia commonly spend a lot of time homeless in part because "[t]hey dislike the diagnosis even more than the idea of being out on the street, because for them the idea of being 'crazy'" is worse. Additionally, Luhrmann wrote that "Indian families don't treat people with schizophrenia as if they have a soul-destroying illness." This from Tanya Luhrmann, who like Justin Barrett, has dedicated a good chunk of her career to dismissing the potential validity of religious beliefs.

Even as outcomes in our country for disease like schizophrenia and bipolar disorder deteriorate, I suggest that people who have nominally dedicated their careers to alleviating these conditions would be unlikely to question materialism, and in particular, to consider premodern approaches to these problems. For modern intellectuals questioning the scientific vision of life is apparently not an option.

5. Considering Evolutionary Challenges

I finish off this chapter on the missing heritability situation by providing a little introduction to the associated evolutionary context. The underlying dynamics of life should ultimately be consistent with the dynamics that led up to the present realities. The contemporary problem connecting DNA to innate outcomes should then have posed historical complications as well.

Continuing, Ernst Mayr's *What Evolution Is* captured some of that potential evolutionary significance with regards to behaviors. In it Mayr again wrote:

> [t]here are reasons to believe that behavioral shifts have been involved in most evolutionary innovations, hence the saying "behavior is the pacemaker of evolution." Any behavior that turns out to be of evolutionary significance is likely to be reinforced by the selection of genetic determinants for such behavior (known as the *Baldwin effect*).[Mayr 2001, p.137].

Thus, innate behaviors should have DNA origins and moreover such genetic origins likely had resonances with natural selection. Those resonances should have had evolutionary impacts too. In a general example, some speciations (or species-creating) events are believed to have been driven by behavioral differentiation. In fact among the Hawaiian genus of crickets, Laupala, there appear to be 38 separate species and the distinguishing aspect amongst them is the males' mating song along with the corresponding females' song preference [Herron and Freeman, pp.625-6]. Those songs consists of very simple series of pulses and the distinguishing feature appears to be the pulse rate. Somehow then the collection of Hawaiian Laupala crickets during their evolution apparently binned or segregated themselves off on the basis of males 'mating call frequencies! Of significance here is that this simple behavioral dynamic - presumed of course to reflect underlying DNA differences - has "astonishing[ly]" evaded efforts to isolate its genetic basis.

Preceding the recent genome searches, though, there are well established DNA origins, in particular for a number of particular disorders and physical features. Beyond some relatively common conditions such as sickle cell anemia, as James D. Watson *et al* pointed out there are "vast numbers of single-gene disorders - the current genetic disease database lists several thousand - but the majority are extremely rare, each occurring in just a few families" [Watson 2017, p.337]. The current confirmed DNA-heritability situation might then be outlined as sporadic successes set against unfolding broad failures in the realms of behavior and health tendencies. One might also infer a genetic basis for the overall layout of bodies since monozygotic twins often have very similar appearances and as earlier alluded to offspring can visibly mirror some features of their parents. Together, this then suggests that either the unfolding heritability failures reflect major flaws in genetic analyses, or that the failures in fact characterize the limited functioning of DNA.

Before exploring evolutionary challenges there are some basic observations about DNA worthy of consideration. It appears that the dynamics of evolution have modified DNA in a haphazard way. Thus for example the enormous variability in the size of genomes found in different organisms [Herron and Freeman, pp.582-91]. Consider again that an onion or a broad-footed salamander which have genomes five and fifty times larger than the human genome, respectively. Additionally, estimates of the functional part of our own genomes are quite low - only 8 percent in one estimate [Zimmer]. Furthermore, substantial ambiguity is implied in the workings of DNA. This is observable in the divergence of monozygotic twins (bolstered by the apparent limits of environmental contributions), and further in the variability of symptoms expressed by the bearers of some disease-correlated alleles. Such variability is termed penetrance or variable expressivity. These two phenomena - DNAs haphazardness and ambiguity - appear to be at odds with the type of precision necessary for a number of DNA's evolutionary roles.

5.a. - Primate Color Vision

One relatively straightforward example of an evolutionary dynamic is considered here. As described in a fine *Scientific American* article, "The Evolution of Primate Color Vision", the outlines of the historical development of the trichromacy in old world primates seems to be understood [Jacobs and Nathan 2007]. This transformation has facilitated the improved color vision of old world primates (including humans). Thus instead of mammalian's common two distinct visual pigments, the eyes of old world primates have three - and thus trichromacy. That transformation apparently involved a sequence of errors in the processing of DNA by which the original (mammalian) two pigment genes were changed into three (the details appear to have entailed some mutations followed by a recombination error). That updated DNA, as demonstrated in some impressive experiments with mice, allowed for better distinguishing of the color spectrum. For reasons perhaps including improvements in the ability to distinguish ripe fruit, this genetic update was likely a natural selection winner and as a result it spread over time. What is of note here is that the requisite physics were not complicated. Some changes in a stretch of primate DNA molecules produced an additional blueprint for a pigment that in turn could be utilized in retinas to significant effect. The resulting improved optical response came directly from the new pigment which in turn was beget directly by the new gene. This historical dynamic certainly appears to be plausible. Behavioral updates on the other hand, would seem to require much more complicated DNA updates to produce coherent changes in brain function.

5.b. - Wasps versus Cockroaches and Other Instinctive Behaviors

The example considered here comes from a lively *Scientific American* article, "Attack of the Zombie Maker" [Catania 2021]. The article chronicles Professor Kenneth Catania's investigation into the remarkable reproductive behaviors of emerald jewel wasps. Those wasps carry out amazing (and brutal) takeovers of American cockroaches in order to facilitate the feeding and development of their larva. While investigating these remarkable attacks Catania also inadvertently observed and then studied an additional phenomenon. The wasps' attack process, like the also impressive defensive response observed on the part of some American cockroaches, is believed to be a genetic programming-based, unlearned routine.

Catania began his article with a quotation from the 1979 horror movie, *Alien*. That quote offered by an android was with regards to that movie's evil creature. In it, it suggested that:

> [y]ou still don't understand what you're dealing with, do you? Perfect organism. Its structural perfection

> is matched only by its hostility…I admire its purity. A survivor, unclouded by conscience, remorse or delusions of morality.

In the movie the alien took over human bodies so that they could provide for the development of its offspring. The somewhat analogous emerald jewel wasp takeover of a cockroach body also provides the requisite circumstances for the wasp's larva. By performing this the jewel wasp is classified as a parasitoid.

Catania introduces his subject by reviewing what earlier observations had uncovered about the jewel wasp's attack on an American cockroach. That attack begins by:

> paralyzing its host, first stinging the cockroach directly in a part of the central nervous system called the first thoracic ganglion. This structure houses the motor neurons that control the roach's front legs. The wasp's venom contains gamma-aminobutyric acid (GABA), an inhibitory neurotransmitter that shuts down the motor neurons, temporarily paralyzing the legs. This first surgical strike leaves the roach unable to protect its head from the next sting, which the wasp directs through the soft membranes of the roach's throat and straight into its brain. The second dose of venom has the insidious effect of changing the roach from a violently struggling (and dangerous) opponent into a compliant and pacified host - that is, a zombie. From there things go predictably downhill for the roach.

That second wasp sting's venom includes the neurotransmitter dopamine which appears to cause the cockroach to focus on grooming itself as opposed to trying to escape.

The emerald jewel wasp then goes and searches for a place to store the disabled cockroach. When the wasp returns to the incapacitated victim it then "grasps one of the roach's sensitive antenna and bites off most of its length". Next, this process is repeated with the other antenna. The resulting bleeding antennae stumps then are effectively used as straws by the wasp in order to replenish itself with the victim's blood. The jewel wasp then drags its prey by one of the antenna stumps into the identified tomb and additionally glues a single egg onto one of the roach's legs. Finally, the wasp seals the roach victim in the tomb.

Professor Catania summarized this remarkably brutal takeover routine with:

> Take a moment to consider this astounding product of evolution. For any predator, it is plenty hard to stalk, catch and kill elusive prey. The emerald jewel wasp has an even greater challenge - taking its prey prisoner so it can serve as a living larder for the larva when it eventually hatches. To do so, the jewel wasp must deliver venom to two small neural targets inside the armored body of an insect that specializes in escaping from threats.

This implies an incredible shaping of innate behavior via natural selection acting on emerald jewel wasp's DNA. I suggest here that no one understands how this could happen.

Additionally, Catania found out there are even more details to the jewel wasp's takeover routine. It turns out that the two sting routine is apparently not sufficient for the productive placement of the egg. After hatching, the resulting larva is quite feeble and thus unlikely to be able to find a viable opening into the body of the cockroach. As a result a mother wasp has to further manipulate the victim in order to glue the egg in a precise spot where the larva can subsequently penetrate the roach's armor. This requires the wasp to sting a third time, this time in the roach's second thoracic ganglion. This particular sting (with its associated venom) causes the roach to extend one of its middle legs. That movement in turn exposes what seems to be a prime location for the placement of the egg.

A further phenomenon in the wasp-versus-cockroach encounter was also uncovered. Catania also noticed that in some cases an American cockroach responds by assuming an effective defensive position involving standing tall on its legs (Catania deemed it the "stilt-standing posture"). With that posture the cockroach can effectively square up to the attacking jewel wasp. One subsequent defending action was noted as quite effective, that is using its long legs to sidekick the wasp in the head. Such kicks had a quite an impact, knocking the wasp "through the air until it crashed into the nearest object". After taking a few such kicks a wasp usually calls off the attack.

Again, these actions by the insects are all presumed to be unlearned instinctive behaviors. There is no evidence that the wasps are schooled in their very elaborate attack procedure or that some of the cockroaches picked up their defensive tactics as a result of attending self-defense classes.

I consider a little further here the emerald wasp's attack routine. The third level of the attack involves the final sting and also the strategic larva placement. Perhaps this final detail could be seen as having evolved in response to some kind of defensive development on the part of American cockroaches. Thus, the third level in accordance with evolution's logic would have likely taken shape in the form of selecting out variable DNA (alleles) in such a way as to accurately carryout the third sting and also to correctly place the larva. Note that such a natural selection dynamic would also face significant constraints in that those selected variants should not interfere with existing vital functions of the wasp, including those specifying for the first two levels of the egg-laying attack. Even skimping a on some details - Catania also observed the jewel wasp somehow utilizes its own abdominal hair as a means to place the larva - this seems very unlikely.

Additional amazing instincts exists as well. Some birds have been shown to demonstrate an innate knowledge of their migration routes, which even the Nobel laureate James D. Watson found astonishing [Watson 2003]. A number of animals

- including dung beetles - appear to utilize the positions of nighttime stars in order to navigate [Sokol]! From a scientific perspective does it really appear possible that a molecule - deoxyribonucleic acid (DNA) - could be shaped by natural selection to encode for the making of a brain so precisely enhanced for navigation? Finally, the domestication of wolves and/or foxes and then subsequent behavioral differentiation of dog breeds, pose quite significant challenges to genetic plausibility as well [Trut and Dugatkin; Watson 2017, pp.386-7].

◆ ◆ ◆

I close this chapter noting two points with regard to the missing heritability problem. One is suggesting that if an analogous impasse were encountered by an alternative and/or religious understanding of life it would likely have drawn considerable attention. In fact, such an unfolding failure might have become a source of ridicule, at least among the more strident followers of science. On the other hand, when materialism hits a major obstacle it seems to draw almost no interest, in particular from academics. Who is willing to question genetics and with it materialism in a big way?

Finally, it is noteworthy that this genetic deficit could be consistent with the intuition offered by the (Nobel laureate) physicist Eugene Wigner with regard to a possible conflict or contradiction at the intersection of the "laws of heredity and of physics" [Wigner].

Chapter 3 - An Introduction to Religions Via Experiences of Self/Ego Transcendence

1. Experiences of Unity or Transcendence

The first two chapters pointed to problems with the scientific vision of life. In some cases the problems are suggestive of some of the dualistic positions common to religions and mystical traditions. Our innate spiritual or religious beliefs are certainly a prominent example of this. Gross indirect support comes from the missing heritability problem which undercuts the molecular determinism assumed by science.

This chapter focuses on profound transformational spiritual/religious experiences, and in particular considers these as offering additional dualistic support and also providing new avenues for meaning. These experiences are significant components of many religious and certainly mystical traditions, and they appear to involve a release from our ordinary ego-based and strife-oriented disposition. As a result of such transformational experiences an individual's self-understanding and psychological orientation tends to be shifted in a helpful way. In some traditions these shifts are also purported to be helpful with regard to subsequent rebirths and in helping others with their sequential life journeys.

Note here that there is a shift away from the idea of a place (some form of heaven) as a final goal. Instead I am focusing on a state of understanding as being a possible big religious/spiritual goal, although conceivably that state might follow from residency in some divine location. Additionally, the religion that I am familiar with, Mahayana Buddhism, has its own somewhat heaven-like rebirth goals [Thondup]. A basic point here, though, is that with real life transformations there is the possibility of getting a glimpse of the deeper aspirations associated with religions.

I go on to suggest here that such remarkable transformations could reflect a grasping of the perspective of an underlying soul (or spirit or simply ultimate Self). With such an interpretation spiritual transformations could offer some support for the dualistic views of religions or simply dualism (here implying at minimum the existence of an underlying soul). A related point here is that it appears that finding phenomena that seem consistent with the presence of a soul is not difficult. On the other hand, arguing for the top-down or God-oriented aspect, seems to be quite challenging. I thus tend to think of these two as constituting the easy and not-easy aspects of religions.

Another possible shift in perspective considered here is that within a reincarnation framework, it could be argued that eternal life is a given. The challenge would be what to do with such a life? Furthermore, this chapter will also in tandem critique the transcendence phenomenon via its depiction in what might be termed Western/Scientific Buddhism. I will largely utilize Sam Harris' book, *Waking Up*, for that somewhat detailed comparison. A basic point made herein, that Western Buddhism has become distorted and superficial, could also apply to the contemporary status of other religions.

Finally, I add here that there are of course many other religions and spiritual perspectives available, but I try here to focus where I have a little familiarity. For those looking for broad coverage of major religions I believe that Huston Smith's *The World Religions* is outstanding [Smith]. I also add that Smith's opening chapter on Hinduism seems particularly noteworthy. Hinduism therein is reported to offer 4 different approaches to self transcendence (or what might be termed encountering a divine consciousness). The first two are termed

Jnana yoga and *Bhakti yoga* and they reflect internal searches (often meditative) and focusing one's love or admiration on God, respectively. Smith also uses the expressions "The Way to God through Knowledge" and "The Way to God through Love", respectively, in describing these two paths. The Buddhist experiences reported on herein appear to be consistent with *Jnana yoga*, while many other religions - including Christianity and parts of Buddhism - appear more consistent with the *Bhakti yoga*. Smith's vast knowledge about religions supported discussions on how these (and other approaches) might lead to similar transformations.

2. *And There Was Light*

The start here will attempt to minimize any connection to established religions/spiritual traditions. Any such connection could taint an individual's descriptions as well as perhaps elicit an ego contribution. I will do this by turning to the "Memoir of a Blind Hero of the French Resistance in World War II", the portrayal of young Jacques Lusseyran in *And There Was Light* [Lusseyran]. In addition to the cover's subtitle (in which "Hero" was presumably the publisher's contribution) I also use an arguably apt description from the back cover. Therein it is written, "one of the most powerful and insightful descriptions of living and thriving with blindness, or indeed any challenge, ever published". It is a remarkable book.

I continue in a quote-full way to include the opening setoff page:

> When you said to me: "Tell me the story of your life," I was not eager to begin. But when you added, "What I care most about is learning your reasons for loving life," then I became eager, for that was a real subject.

> All the more since I have maintained this love of life through everything: through infirmity, the terrors of war, and even in Nazi prisons. Never did it fail me, not in misfortune nor in good times, which may seem much easier but is not.
>
> Now, it is no longer a child who is going to tell this story and that is regrettable. It is a man. Worse yet, it is the university professor I have become. I will have to guard myself very carefully from trying to expound and demonstrate - those two illusions. I will have to return to the simplicity of a child ...

As evident above, Lusseyran in addition to trying to layout some profound inner dynamics, also offered some welcome sober commentary with regard to the pitfalls of adulthood. After an accident at school left him blind at age 7, Lusseyran somehow came upon an inner light which transformed his life and even somehow left him with a simple form of vision. He wrote that this realization got started as he "began to look more closely, not at things but at a world closer to myself, looking from an inner place to one further within". Perhaps this was indirectly facilitated by circumstances as he "instead of clinging to the movement of sight toward the world outside" became more inwardly aware [Lusseyran, p.11].

As this happened his perception seemed to shift and he came upon a surprising inner light. He found this to be an:

> indescribable relief, and happiness so great it almost made me laugh. Confidence and gratitude came as if a prayer had been answered. I found light and joy at the same moment, and can say without hesitation that from that time on light and joy have never been separated in my experience. I have had them or lost them together [p.11].

Science's Dead End, Religions' Opening, and a Restart for Meaning

Somehow he seemed to have crossed a threshold and was subsequently able to experiment and extend this novel inner connection or capacity. At times he interpreted this development as an unearned gift from God and for years Lusseyran considered it to be his secret.

Amidst a description of some of his wide-ranging conversations with his close friend, Jean, Lusseyran also described the change in his perspective that came with his inner light revelation. In another long quote:

> I explained to him that it was a preconceived idea which made the process [rebounding from introversion] hard for him - an idea, by the way, which almost everyone shares - that there are two worlds - one without, the other within. I kept having to explain all over again because Jean wanted to believe me but couldn't. The preconceived idea always stood in the way.
>
> We talked about this at least once a week in the frame of mind of people going to Mass on Sunday. After all, it was a religious subject. The reality - the oneness of the world - left me in the lurch, incapable of explaining it, because it seemed obvious. I could only repeat: 'there is only one world. Things outside only exist if you go to meet them with everything you carry in yourself. As to the things inside, you will never see them well unless you allow those outside to enter in.'
>
> To pass from the inner light to the light of the sun was not the work of the senses. A click sufficed, a slight change in point of view, like turning one's head a hundredth part of a circle. It was enough in the end to believe. The rest came by itself.

> To convince Jean (which mattered terribly to me) I assembled all my arguments. If he wanted to be completely happy, there must be only one world, for this was the indispensable condition.
>
> This joy was well known to me. It was the Grace of my state of being. When I read in the gospels that the Word was made Flesh, I told myself that this was indeed true. At the same time I was aware that I had done nothing to deserve it. It had simply been given to me, and I prayed God that Jean, too, should receive it [pp.76-7].

Somehow Lusseyran, although unschooled in mystical or religious ways, had stumbled onto what might be termed a Unity state. His encounter wasn't a transient event, instead he somehow got a foothold and in fact quite a bit of the book chronicled his efforts at integrating the transformation into his daily life.

I add a possible physical analogy to Lusseyran's light connection. Anyone who rides a bicycle maintains a subtle but tangible connection to their sense of balance. Cyclists might have numerous conscious decisions to make (safety demands this), but conscious effort with regards to balance is somehow not required. As a beginner you pick this up and then allow it to function as per the dynamic requirements of subsequent cycling. On the other hand, if a cyclist consciously tried to control their balance I suspect it would be dangerous. It is somehow a subtle but vital process or connection. I suggest that Lusseyran's inner light (or state of grace) connection might have been a little analogous to this.

Lusseyran also communicated the fragile and subtle character of his inward connection. Any strong contrary focuses - such as impatience, anger, jealousy, or fear - faded the connection and the transcendent vision was then replaced by "fog or smoke" [p.15]. (Thankfully a cyclist's balance is not as sensitive to mental commotion.) This visual dynamic "took the place of red and green [moral] lights" and left him loving "friendship and harmony" [p.15]. His ongoing maintenance of morality then perhaps relied on feedback from his inner light connection.

The main messages conveyed in his book were of both a subtle inward possibility and more tangibly, its apparent big effect on Lusseyran's life. He accomplished extraordinary things all the way through his stay in Buchenwald concentration camp. The book's final paragraph summarized his revelations with two claims which he believed were general:

> The first of these is that joy does not come from outside, for whatever happens to us is within. The second truth is that light does not come to us from without. Light is in us, even if we have no eyes [p.280].

I go on here to suggest that Lusseyran's light and revelations could offer corroborating evidence for the existence of the type of transformations that some traditions emphasize. From my knowledge of Buddhism, Lusseyran's revelation appear to have been roughly consistent with the goal of an enlightenment experience. Along those lines it is perhaps noteworthy that in the *Tibetan Book of the Dead* it is suggested that this "mind of yours is inseparable luminosity and emptiness in the form of a great mass of light, it has no birth or death" [Fremantle and Trungpa: p.87]. That *Tibetan Book of the Dead* description might then also offer an elemental description of the soul.

Lusseyran's experience might then be viewed as an encounter with the soul, or at least a subtle grasping of its perspective. His experience also points to our latent potential for deeper joy and meaning in our lives. Lusseyran's revelation was ultimately significant due to the resulting transformation, as opposed to some kind of novel psychological experience (which we all have) which might then beget some form of spiritualized intellectualizations [Lightman]. Additionally, Lusseyran used some Christian terms to describe his breakthrough. He also had had some exposure to his father's role in the Anthroposophical Society with their interest in the mystic Rudolph Steiner whose teachings included reincarnation. In all, these may have contributed to Lusseyran's take on his revelation. But the way this happened and Lusseyran's subsequent matter-of-factness about his life appear to leave his experience as well characterized. Even Oliver Sacks was quoted on the book as "[m]ost beautiful".

3. Buddhism, Enlightenment, and Sam Harris' Waking Up

I transition here to commentary with regard to Sam Harris' book, *Waking Up*, and with it the modern transformation of the religion Buddhism. Such a makeover might have contemporary parallels in other religions. In his book Harris attempted to strip out the "metaphysical ideas … [of] ignorant and isolated people of the past" [Harris, p.33] and ultimately offer a science-kosher guide to studying your consciousness via meditation, with a particular aim on "self-transcendence" or enlightenment. I also suggest that the commentary here is indirectly relevant to the contemporary hegemony of science. Furthermore, it also touches on some matters that could be useful in the general search for meaning.

As an introductory synopsis, Harris missed many essentials. The secularization efforts of the book were neither novel nor necessary. In the West, Buddhist practice has for decades been pushed in a largely areligious fashion, along with significant efforts to tie the practice to scientific and intellectual perspectives. Additionally, significant enlightenment experiences are very rare and thus the rigors of traditional monastic practice. If Harris' points about the efficacy of meditation and also drugs for personal transformation were accurate then they should be self-evident given the cumulative involvement with both in the West. Also the scientific certainty with which he built his materialist arguments did not exist at the time of publication (2014), or now.

◆ ◆ ◆

I initially provide a little of my own relevant background. I have been involved with daily Buddhist's practices (including meditation) for over 40 years. Unlike Sam Harris, I am not a philosophically-oriented person. My ongoing interests in dealing with the challenges of life (for myself and others) has reinforced that tendency.

Towards the end of the book Harris' stated the basic objective of *Waking Up*:

> [u]ntil we can talk about spirituality in rational terms - acknowledging the validity of self-transcendence - our world will remain shattered by dogmatism. This book has been my attempt to begin such a conversation [p.203].

This quote is a good place to begin to see the kind of nonsense going on in this popular science-framed book. First off, dogmatism is symptomatic of human rigidity and it is omnipresent and regularly divisive. One of the appealing messages coming out of what might be termed scientism is that you can simply shun religion and embrace (or nod your head to) science and you are good to go in a largely unencumbered conceptual sense. Apparently in some quarters religion ruins everything and followers of science on the other hand are somehow freethinkers (despite science's lack of support for free will). In fact as humans we can get rigidly hung up anywhere. A prominent gross example is the super-rigid nature of political discourse.

At no point in his book did Harris acknowledge the work of the neurologist and longtime Zen practitioner, James H. Austin. Austin had written a series of books trying to make neural/materialist sense out of Zen practice, including his own enlightenment experience (apparently an introductory or kensho experience). His writings are extensive and were published via MIT Press. Amongst the wide range of topics in his first book, *Zen and the Brain: Toward an Understanding of Meditation and Consciousness*, Austin included a critical look at drug experiences [Austin]. In total, as of my earlier page-counting effort it appears that Austin had published 2,140 pages before *Waking Up* was published.

Harris might be excused for omitting this earlier extensive work, since James Austin was not (and I assume still is not) a celebrity author. But this apparent oversight is the tip of the problem here. At no point in my previous scouring of Austin's writings have I seen evidence that Austin even acknowledged the underlying religious/metaphysical framework (specifically life-after-life) of Buddhist's practice including Zen. But for someone who has followed the Western Buddhist - or for the most part, Buddhist-derivative - contemporary scene, Austin's oversight was not surprising. For as long as I have been involved with Buddhist practice the overwhelming tendency has been to pretend around its religious beliefs and framework. Thus Buddhism in the West did not need Harris (or anyone else) to introduce the conversation because the secularization tendency has largely been the default process for decades. In a physical sense it appears that many involved Westerners have treated the marginally incorporated religious aspects of Buddhism like people in general treat gift wrapping. You pull it off, throw it out (or attempt to recycle it), and then forget it.

I introduce another point from Austin's work before moving on. James Austin was strongly motivated by a big question - how is it that a short term internal experience can apparently have long term positive consequences? From a materialist perspective that is the big question surrounding experiences like enlightenment. Somehow such brief events appear capable of engendering significant positive psyche changes (as with Lusseyran). For historical support here I suggest that the long record of serious meditational efforts in part reflects this phenomenon. People have observed such changes in others and pursue meditation hoping for their own transformations. Austin opened his *Zen and the Brain* with his "straightforward thesis" that "[deep] awakening, enlightenment occurs only because the human brain undergoes substantial changes" which were suggested to "both profoundly enhance yet simplify, the working of the brain" [Austin, p.xix]. Austin's book stepped up and attempted to provide a brain-based answer which was the materialist thing to do, although clearly not an easy task. The brain, like the rest of the body, is susceptible to transient events inflicting serious setbacks, but the plausibility of short term lasting enhancement is difficult to grasp. Harris's book should have also addressed this question.

I will hit pause here on Harris' supposed conversation-starting. For a little background on Buddhism and meditation I briefly present some points from the academics, Robert E. Buswell, Jr. and Donald S. Lopez, Jr., as described in their article "10 Misconceptions about Buddhism" [Buswell and Lopez]. The first of their misconceptions is that "All Buddhists meditate" which the authors rebutted in part with "[m]editation has traditionally been considered a monastic practice, and even then, a speciality only of certain monks". The effectiveness of meditation again tends to be overstated in the West and Harris stayed consistent with this.

Buswell and Lopez's next three misconceptions were relatively minor - "[t]he primary form of Buddhist meditation is mindfulness"; all "Buddhists are vegetarians"; and all "Buddhists are pacifists". The fifth misconception was a big one, though, "Buddhism is a philosophy and not a religion". In its entirety this entry read:

> Buddhism has many philosophical schools, with a sophistication equal to that of any philosophical school that developed in Europe. However, Buddhism is a religion, by any definition of that indefinable term, unless one defines religion as a

> belief in a creator God. The great majority of Buddhist practice over history, for both monks and laypeople, has been focused on obtaining a good rebirth in the next lifetime, whether for oneself, one's family, or for all beings in the universe.

This is a prevalent misconception about Buddhism as it is interpreted in the West and Harris should have stated this. The religious framework of Buddhism could well have been inherited in part from premodern life-after-life beliefs. Buddhist practices including meditation were ultimately designed to help people better deal with the challenges associated with serial living.

The sixth misconception was, "[t]he Buddha was a human being, not a god, and the religion he founded has no place for the worship of gods". This is probably where secular spokespersons like Harris would like it. Here Buswell and Lopez's entry was:

> Buddhism has an elaborate pantheon of celestial beings (devas, etymologically related to the English word "divinity") and advanced spiritual beings (bodhisattvas and buddhas), who occupy various heavens and pure lands and who respond to the prayers of the devout.

Religions are probably more alike than commonly thought.

Next, on the presumed anti-religious form of Buddhism, Zen, the authors had an entry titled, "Zen rejects conventional Buddhism. Zen masters burn statues of the Buddha, scorn the sutras [teaching of the Buddha], and regularly frequent bars and brothels". Harris made a few derogatory comments about Zen but missed its minimalistic appeal. If you really want a this-life-only oriented practice, then Zen - certainly as it has been commonly practiced in the West - appears pretty optimal. Here the entry was:

Zen monks follow a strict set of regulations, called "pure rules," which are based on the monastic discipline imported from India. Most Zen monks have engaged in extensive study of Buddhist scriptures before beginning their training in the meditation hall. And although one of the Four Phrases of Zen is "not relying on words and letters," Zen has the largest body of written literature of any tradition within East Asian Buddhism.

A basic point minimized in *Waking Up* is that discipline and morality tend to be vital contributors to the potential helpfulness of meditational practices. The "quality of one's mind" and with it one's meditation practice is significantly shaped by the quality of one's actions. This general point about the import of discipline and morality should be self-evident to any adult. Another basic goal of Buddhist practice is to try to build a helpful or compassionate inclination towards other beings. Within Mahayana Buddhism that desired inclination is sometimes termed bodhicitta and it is believed to be an important contributor to the potential for meaningful transformation.

The ninth misconception also happened to be dedicated to Zen and in its entirety was (with the opening line here being the title-misconception):

> Zen is dedicated to the experience of "sudden enlightenment," which frees its followers from the extended regimens of training in ethics, meditation, and wisdom found in conventional forms of Buddhism. Zen monks routinely expect to spend decades in full-time practice before they will be able to make real progress in their meditation.

The last point here is a rebut to the contemporary optimism about the ease of meditational progress and thus the likeliness of the goal in *Waking Up*. This point also highlights the apparent uniqueness of Jacque Lusseyran's experience.

♦ ♦ ♦

Harris should certainly have provided an example of a meditation-based enlightenment experience as this is the central focus of his book. Here I provide an enlightenment (or Self-realization) account as given in an introduction to Zen practice, *Three Pillars of Zen* [Kapleau, pp.215-9] (a book which is rather unique in containing several enlightenment accounts). The following excerpts were written by a Japanese executive in the 1950's. In an initial note to his Zen teacher the executive had written:

> You remember the discussion which arose about Self-realization centering around that American. At that time I hardly imagined that in a few days I would be reporting to you my own experience.

The executive went on to describe that during the train ride home from the monastery with his wife, he had been deeply struck whilst reading a passage from Zen literature. The particular passage read was "I came to realize clearly that Mind is no other than mountains and rivers and the great wide earth, the sun and the moon and the stars".

This passage somehow deeply resonated with this man and his meditational experiences. During the subsequent days it triggered an enlightenment experience (in the awkward company of his family and brother and sister-in-law). During his first night home he wrote that:

> [a]t midnight I abruptly awakened. At first my mind was foggy, then suddenly that quotation flashed into my consciousness: "I came to realize that Mind is no other than mountains, rivers, and the great wide earth, the sun and the moon and the stars". And I repeated it. Then all at once I was struck as though by lightening, and the next instant heaven and earth crumbled and disappeared. Instantly, like surging

waves, a tremendous delight welled up in me, a veritable hurricane of delight, as I laughed wildly and loudly: "Ha, ha, ha, ha, ha, ha! There's no reasoning here, no reasoning at all! Ha, ha, ha!" The empty sky split in two, then opened its mouth and began to laugh uproariously: "Ha, ha, ha!".

The executive then went on to exclaim, "I've come to enlightenment! Shakyamuni [i.e., the Buddha] and the patriarchs have not deceived me!" This revelatory experience then got a bit awkward as his family was clueless about his inner experiences so the executive downshifted and apologized for his outbursts.

The next day the executive went to visit a Zen teacher and he was simply overcome with joy and wept. That teacher reportedly commented, "it is rare indeed to experience to such a wonderful degree. It is termed 'Attainment of the emptiness of Mind'. You are to be congratulated." As a possible crude explanation here, somehow his extensive meditation practice plus the triggering of the quote allowed him to vividly break through the very deeply-entrenched, me-and-the-world story that we operate within. Also of note here is that the conceptual nature of his revelation seems roughly consistent with Lusseyran's assertion that "the world is one".

His enlightenment breakthrough continued across the next few days and left him "laughing and weeping" extensively. The executive then contacted his original teacher in hopes of offering some inspiration to his monks and also in hopes of helping the novice American. To the latter he suggested letting him know that "even I, who am unworthy and lacking in spirit, can grasp such a wonderful experience when time matures". He further suggested telling that American - who not surprisingly was hoping for enlightenment within a week - that, "don't say days, weeks, or even lifetimes. Don't say millions of billions of kalpa. Tell him to vow to attain enlightenment though it takes the infinite, the boundless, the incalculable future". A kalpa is an extremely long period of time.

The executive's subsequent diary entries included, "Am totally at peace at peace at peace", "Am supremely free free free free free free", and "The substance of Mind - this is now luminously clear to me". And finally in a concluding paragraph he wrote that:

> The ancients said the enlightened mind is comparable to a fish swimming. That's exactly how it is - there's no stagnation. I feel no hinderance. Everything flows smoothly, freely. Everything goes naturally. This limitless freedom is beyond all expression. What a wonderful world.

The executive finally stated simply, "I am grateful, so grateful."

Of note here is that an enlightenment or transformational experience like the above is simply not on the radar screen of science. Along those lines, years ago in talking with a highly educated physicist they simply categorized such revelations as episodes of schizophrenia or craziness. They certainly don't make equation-sense. A further note is that such an experience might tend to be a bigger breakthrough for an adult than for a young child. I doubt Lusseyran's grasping of an underlying unity state was accompanied by the seeming excesses of this businessman. As adults we are probably much more grooved into our mental me-ruts or -routines.

For some further perspective on enlightenment (and perhaps other profound religious or mystical breakthroughs) one might consider that the underlying soul relinquishes identification with the brain's activities. Such a release could then be characterized as liberation from entanglement with the material aspects of consciousness. Perhaps along these lines the coauthor of the *Tibetan Book of the Dead*, Tibetan Buddhist teacher Chogyam Trungpa mentioned in his commentary that "[w]hen energy becomes independent, complete energy, it begins to look at itself, which transcends the ordinary idea of perception" [Fremantle and Trungpa, p.29].

Continuing, some of the most lucid descriptions of the enlightened state or terrain that I have seen are in the far-reaching conversations with the Indian Advaita Vedanta (Hindu-connected) teacher, Sri Nisargadatta Maharaj, found in the aptly entitled book *I AM THAT* [Nisargadatta]. One of Nisargadatta's basic points is that once you can clearly observe ordinary consciousness at work that perception opens the door to a deeper experience of life and self. That experience could then be enlightenment. In one succinct exchange with a student Nisargadatta suggests that by reigning in excessive imagination and attachment we are then able to "see [reality] as it is, not through the screen of desire and fear" [Nisargadatta, p.286].

An additional point here is that significant experiences are very rare and almost inevitably come after long dedicated practice. Harris claims that the Dzogchen teacher he visited, Tulko Urgyen Rinpoche, matter of factly brought him to enlightenment and moreover could do so for others. If anything like this was true then Harris' description of that experience would likely be profound; there would have been a mile-long line at Tulku Urgyen's door; and the actual training associated with (Tibetan Buddhisms') Dzogchen practice would not be such a long, rigorous, and largely monastic affair. This tendency to trivialize Dzogchen in the West in fact got one of Sam Harris' former teachers, the westerner Lama Surya Das, denounced by their former Tibetan teacher.

Continuing with some enlightenment commentary, I have been around some serious practitioners, including monastic figures, my sense is that such transformations really are profound and potentially have lasting impacts (as with Lusseyran). In simple physical terms it is as though the default condition as human beings were to walk around with pebbles in our shoes. Spiritual liberation or enlightenment in that analogy is when a person finds a way to shed the pebbles. Thus, I have sensed in others that via significant meditational practice and an enlightenment experience, they are somehow considerably more at ease with life and themselves.

I add two more references here of potential interest to readers. The first is of an even deeper enlightenment experience that also happened in Japan. That experience happened to a very sick young Japanese woman, Yaeko Iwasaki, in the 1930's and is described in Chapter 6 of Kapleau's *The Three Pillars of Zen*. The inherent sense of responsibility, humility, and deeper perspective on life and death apparently beget by her liberation experience are noteworthy. Additionally, after amazingly marching through a sequence of breakthroughs in only a week, Iwasaki came to realize the significance of deep enlightenment experiences and also accept her pending death (which she sensed coming).

A second reference that might be of interest involves the story of a contemporary Japanese man, Ittetsu Nemoto, who plunged into traditional (and barely still existing) monastic Rinzai Zen training and then subsequently dedicated himself to helping out with suicide prevention efforts in Japan. A fine article, *The Last Call*, describing this was published in the *New Yorker* magazine and was written by Larissa MacFarquhar [MacFarquhar]. Nemoto's journey is notable for a number of reasons. He managed in his very intense journey to stay clear of two meditational tendencies - the first is too much withdrawal and secondly his apparent lack of interest in intellectualizing (Nemoto is apparently no Sam Harris). But MacFarquhar's article nicely portraits Nemoto's extremely rigorous training; seemingly miraculous enlightenment experience; serious dedication to helping in the outside world; and also his sober conclusion that we learn and are potentially transformed through suffering - and likely intense suffering at that.

◆ ◆ ◆

Here I will attempt to further convey the unlikeliness of significant enlightenment experiences which Harris even went so far as to attribute to drug usage. I indirectly get started with a self observation. Set against a number of challenges I have experienced there seems to be one mundane constant. That is no matter how derailed I can get, in a basic objective $2 + 2 = 4$ sense I tend to stay grounded. That same nerd tendency surfaced itself for years within the Western Buddhist scene where the availability of enlightenment experiences tend to be greatly oversold.

In a possibly parallel perspective a Western meditation teacher, A. H. Almaas, had written:

> [a] realized teacher might have thousands of students but it is rare if even a handful of them actually attain liberation [Almaas, p.4].

A. H. Almaas had been a physics graduate student when he decided to exit the scientific scene and instead apply himself to meditative inquiry. Also the notable and neglected physicist David Bohm, after spending years in sort of a part-time, supremely-intellectual sidekick role to the spiritual teacher Jiddu Krishnamurti, made the same point about the rarity of significant enlightenment/transformational experiences and suggested this rarity had a long history [Bohm and Peat].

Another very well-grounded assessment of the likelihood of enlightenment was given at the end of the Zen classic, *Zen Teaching of Huang Po*, by John Blofeld [Blofeld]. In it the famous Zen teacher Huang Po commented that:

> Ah be diligent. Be diligent! Of a thousand or ten thousand attempting to enter by this [Zen enlightenment] Gate, only three or perhaps five pass through. If you are heedless of my warnings, calamity is sure to follow. Therefore it is written, "Exert your strength in THIS life to attain! Or else incur long aeons of further [karmic] gain!" [Blofeld, p.132].

Even in a much less distraction-prone era, a practice very much focused on this life, in a likely super-rigorous Zen monastery saw limited success. By comparison, how many modern Western meditational outfits - nominally Buddhist or otherwise - do not grossly oversell the return on meditation and in particular the availability of enlightenment?

As a follow up point, Huang Po is coming from the traditional monastic Zen (in China, Chan) perspective. In it you want to very seriously pursue having a deep enlightenment experience so that you can end your gross dissatisfaction with life (and thus share in something like Lusseyran's grace). That experience is also supposed to free up an individual from the ignorance which drives the compulsions which tend to lead to rebirth. This latter goal does seem to conflict, though, with the oft-stated commitment of helping others in the future and thus returning to help out. In comparison there are other traditional Buddhist practices that are more modest in their ambitions and use simple practices to try to improve your life and also - and this is the religious part - your post-death trajectory including possibly facilitating an enlightenment breakthrough in the disembodied or bardo state. Whereas Huang Po above expressed dismay over the possibility of reincarnating, other Buddhists (certainly some Mahayana Buddhists) appear committed to coming back to help out and also learning more lessons.

◆ ◆ ◆

I add a related parallel point. Years ago when I regularly attended meetings for an anti-(or really reduced)-nuclear weapons group there was another attendee that drew my attention. That attendee was an older man who seemed remarkably at ease with life and himself. Eventually I spoke to the man after one of the meetings and asked him about his background. With my own background and biases I assumed he must have been involved with meditation (and probably for many years at that). But that was not the case. The man reported that he had been involved with a small Christian church. Whatever the vehicle, though, such mystical/religious transformations appear to be rare. A simple point, though, is that based on my observations I feel people can find some benefit, and with it, be beneficial, as a result of their religious/spiritual practices.

I go on to add here that I doubt the accuracy of Sam Harris' presentation of his enlightenment. His teacher-facilitated awakening in fact sounds similar to the woman's (also teacher-facilitated) awakening that he playfully critiqued in his book. He should have acknowledged that there is a lot of pressure on teachers to convey some sense of success if only to have students stick around (and thus for example, the aforementioned A. H. Almaas himself went on to purpose his own unrealistic shortcut method). If awakenings were as commonly available as *Waking Up* suggests then we should know this. Largely secular meditation practices have been pretty widely available for at least 4 decades now, it should be common knowledge that people can find very helpful psyche shifts via meditating. The same situation could be said of drug usage. I do think though that meditation can be helpful in simple ways, starting with its encouragement of paying attention. Additionally, from what I have seen being around drug users I wouldn't even endorse a net helpful there (benefits for some conditions have garnered positive media but I suggest waiting longer for the hoopla to settle). Net effects are what matters and if you can get net positives that is great. The sober nature of life seems to be reflected in that fact that most net positives consist of simply avoiding harmful activities.

A relevant critical look at the contemporary Western Buddhist scene was also present in another *Tricycle* magazine article. That article was by a serious meditation student Eliot Fintushel and from a secular-only perspective it critiqued the state of Western teachers [Fintushel]. What was particularly significant about the writeup was that it was written arguably from the high ground of Western Buddhism. The type of teachers critiqued had had significant meditational training and some enlightenment experiences (like Fintushel). Though possibly well short of traditional Asian standards, these teachers represented quite successful lay outcomes for sustained Buddhist meditational practice in the West. Yet as Fintushel described there appeared to be prevalent problems with loose and selfish behaviors among those teachers. Fintushel went on to suggest that "[i]n each case the devastation was proportional to the teacher's 'charisma'". I add that perhaps a more telling sign of the distortions associated with Western Buddhism showed in an ad along the way (in the magazine version). The ad showed a photo of a prominent American Zen teacher along with the text, "Change your life in an afternoon! Unlock the Zen power in you!". I wonder if having a self-help ceiling on your vision tends to facilitate problems.

◆ ◆ ◆

Sam Harris presented a split brain experiment-based argument for a brain-only vision of our mind or self. He confidently pointed out that such patients can appear in some experiments to have two selves and thus our sense of a unified self (and potentially with it a soul) is a neural-concocted illusion. But he doesn't mention complications to such reasoning. First, in an everyday way we can all experience the presence of apparent multiple selves when caught up in our competing desires. Additionally, in a neural sense the aforementioned work of John Lorber provides counterexamples [Lewin]. When there is good evidence that people can function normally - and even have a high IQ - yet have gross deficiencies in neural volume that challenges neuroscience's assumptions. With approximately 5 percent of normal brain volume how can you neurally support a regular sense of self, let alone the possibility of fragmenting it into two or more selves? Additionally, in Lorber's work the brain-body symmetry assumption of neuroscience was also challenged.

Harris also disregarded two established phenomena (discussed in Chapter 1) that are quite suggestive of the presence and/or influence of additional souls. There is the multiple personality disorder. With people experiencing several largely segregated selves and this occurring without any splitting interventions, how would neuroscience explain that? And with the also described psychological impacts observed in some heart transplant recipients, this also undermines the hypothesis that our mental content follows only from our brain's activities.

Harris' ultimate point with his arguments was of course to rebut the possibility of dualism and thus possible support for religious perspectives. (Although in some official contexts Buddhism is supposed to deny any underlying self - don't ask how). Another unacknowledged challenge to Harris' brain-only point include the aforementioned dualistic spiritual perspectives we appear to be born with. How in a molecular-only (and evolutionary) sense can you explain the existence of such beliefs? And a final obvious challenge the to brain-only/no-soul logic would be with the earlier described terminal lucidity. How can cognitively, and thus presumably neurally, long-gone individuals return to a coherent self and state?

◆ ◆ ◆

Moving along with Sam Harris, he also wrote that:

> [t]here is now a large literature on the psychological benefits of meditation. Different techniques produce long-lasting changes in attention, emotion, cognition, and pain perception, and these correlate with both structural and functional changes in the brain. This field of research is quickly growing, as is our understanding of self-awareness and related phenomena. Given recent advances in neuroimaging technology, we no longer face a practical impediment to investigating spiritual insights in the context of science [Harris, p.8].

But if this were true it should again be apparent in an everyday sense and thus be common knowledge. From my observations "long-lasting changes" in a deep positive sense are simply not easy and are thus rare. Traditionally, meditation largely had a home in monasteries and this likely was to facilitate transformations and then to help stabilize them. Analogous reasoning and efforts may of course have been found in other forms of religious training too.

Roughly contemporary with Harris' above claims was a 2014 *Scientific American* article, "mind of the meditator", by Matthieu Ricard, Antoine Lutz, and Richard J. Davidson [Ricard *et al*]. That neural-meditation article mentioned the associated inspirational efforts of the Dalai Lama. It considered neural imaging changes believed to be associated with three meditational techniques - compassion and loving kindness, mindfulness, and focused attention. The three authors made some claims similar to Harris' with regards to the effects of meditation including:

> [a]bout 15 years of research have done more than show that meditation produces significant changes in both the function and structure of the brains of experienced practitioners. These studies are now starting to demonstrate that contemplative practices may have a substantive impact on biological processes critical for physical health.

Of note here is that "experienced practitioners" implies people with over 10,000 hours of meditation experience. At a rate of an hour a day that translates to over 27 years of daily meditation. The article went on to state:

> [t]he ability to cultivate compassion and other positive qualities lays the foundation for an ethical framework unattached to any philosophy or religion, which could have a profoundly beneficial effect on all aspects of human societies.

But the article seemed loosely quantitative and the one graph which purported to show enhancement in neural features derived from meditation seems to show small effects with significant overlap found between the measurements of experienced meditators and those of controls. The authors also failed to respond to a published follow-up letter from a meditator regarding the possibility that their results could have been distorted by selection bias. How many lay people really have a chance of joining the 10,000 hour club (and thus the possibility of selection bias)?

More seriously, though, why didn't Sam Harris and Matthieu Ricard *et al* acknowledge that secularly-packaged meditation has been pretty widely available in the West for at least 40 years? If such meditation was as self-help productive as suggested in the article by Richard *et al* and also in *Waking Up*, then why didn't that meditation sell itself (like an effective dieting routine likely would have) without the need for promotion by neuroscience? I mentioned that to an older very experienced American meditator and she simply nodded her head in agreement.

In some of my other writings I related some personal experience of the science-bent ways of Buddhism in the West [Christopher 2017a; 2022c]. These in short were roughly consistent with a quote I have used from a Western Buddhist teacher. This teacher claimed that that he and many other modern Buddhists experience "profound embarrassment" over Buddhism's rebirth belief, but satisfaction over Buddhism's apparent "resonance with quantum physics, cutting edge neuroscience, and modern rationality" [Spellmeyer]. For those with an irreverent sense of humor you might consider placing that quote on your refrigerator.

Framing the preceding neuro-meditation works are presumptions about the accuracy of neuroscience. In the period in which Harris (and Richard et al) was writing there were neuroscientists who wrote about the sober state of neuroscience. A 2014 issue of *Scientific American* had a such an article by Rafael

Yuste and George M. Church [Yuste and Church]. Following an optimistic title of "The New Century of the Brain - Big Science lights the way to an understanding of how the world's most complex machine gives rise to our thoughts and emotions", the authors gave a very sober layout of how little is currently known and how much in the way of technical developments appears needed. Such developments would be focused on controlling and recording the activity of the brain's labyrinth of circuits. The authors opened their task by offering a sober example:

> [d]espite a century of sustained research, brain scientists remain ignorant of the workings of the three-pound organ that is the seat of all conscious activity. Many have tried to attack this problem by examining the nervous systems of simpler organisms. In fact, almost 30 years have passed since investigators mapped the connections among each of the 302 nerve cells in the round worm Caenorhabditis elegans. Yet the worm-wiring diagram did not yield an understanding of how these connections give rise to even rudimentary behaviors such as feeding and sex. What was missing were data relating the activity of neurons to specific behaviors.

They went on to point how deceptive and superficial popular presentations of human brain experiments tend to be. Commenting on one popular story, the authors wrote:

> A noteworthy example of the mismatch is a much publicized study identifying single brain cells that fired an electrical impulse in response to the face of actor Jennifer Aniston. Despite the hoopla, the discovery of a "Jennifer Aniston neuron" was something like a message from aliens, a sign of intelligent life in the universe but without any indication about the meaning of the transmission.

We are still completely ignorant of how the pulsing electrical activity of that neuron influences our ability to recognize Aniston's face and then relate it to a clip from the television show *Friends*. For the brain to recognize the star, it probably has to activate a large ensemble of neurons, all communicating using neural code that we have yet to decipher.

On a related note *Scientific American* also had a February 2013 article, "Brain Cells for Grandmother" by the experimenters who had encountered in one patient the apparent "Jennifer Aniston neuron" (which also appeared to respond to another costar from the TV show *Friends*).

Overall, Yuste and Church claimed that for neuroscience to fundamentally advance it:

> needs a new set of technologies that will enable investigators to monitor and also alter the electrical activity of thousands or even millions of neurons - techniques capable of deciphering what the Spanish neuroanatomist Santiago Ramon y Cajal called 'the impenetrable jungles where many investigators have lost themselves'.

Penetrating those jungles, though, as outlined in the Yuste and Church article is likely to be a monumental task. Along the way if researchers can create the requisite technologies then they can scale up the brains examined. Even with a mouse's brain, though, such efforts "could generate 300 terabytes of compressed data in an hour". These enormous challenges led the authors to the plea-full conclusion:

> We need collaboration among academic disciplines. Building instruments to image voltage in millions of neurons simultaneously throughout entire brain regions may be achieved only by a sustained effort of a large interdisciplinary team of researchers. The

technology could then be made available at a large-scale, observatory-like facility shared by the neuroscience community. We are passionate about retaining a focus on new technology to record, control and decode the patterns of electrical spikes that are the language of the brain. We believe that without these new tools, neuroscience will remain bottlenecked and fail to detect the brain's emergent properties that underlie a virtually infinite range of behaviors. Enhancing the ability to understand and use the language of spikes and neurons is the most productive way to derive a grand theory of how nature's most complex machine functions.

Additional complexity appears to have been neglected here, though. In the end whatever is recorded with regards to an individual's brain activity will likely have to be compared against that individual's limited description of their concurrent subjective mental experience. And such an experience would necessarily be a static one within an "observatory-like facility".

Another route to appreciating the limits of brain science's position might be to consider discrete conditions. Three profound conditions standout for the scientific and also public attention they have received - autism, schizophrenia, and Alzheimer's. Of particular note here are their origins. For autism and schizophrenia those are in large part believed to be genetic, and of additional note is their physical (or neural) bases. That is respectively, what causes the conditions, and also what the conditions physically entail. For the presumed genetically driven conditions, schizophrenia and autism, as alluded to previously the genetic searches have seemingly failed; and for all three, perhaps even more remarkably - neuroscience is still appears to be grasping at models in order to describe what is going on in the brain with these conditions.

Finally, I suggest here that a neglected contemporary question is - has the mindfulness *et al* movement, even dented the formidable tsunami of electronic distraction underway in our society? That context was not even mentioned in *Waking Up* or in Ricard *et al*'s article. I think if it were possible to regulate cellphones in such a way as to reduce their usage by a factor of two, that would likely do more to help society's state of mindfulness than whatever goes on within the official mindfulness business. Gross dis-attention appears to be a large and growing problem. I add that I think of screen-time as tending to be the opposite of meditation-, prayer-, or work-time.

Some Conclusions About Meditation and Religious Inquiry

I have been focusing here on meditation but these points might also relate to other religious practices too. The aforementioned Nisargadatta suggested that transformation ultimately doesn't come down to techniques (or cleverness or cliches), it appears to come down to sustained commitment or "earnestness" to learn about ourselves. I think he might have meant that if we are really serious about personal transformation, we will ultimately find our way. This could be consistent with Hinduism's multi-pronged approach.

Continuing, probably the simplest reason to try some meditation is to explore paying attention in a fuller sense. We all pay attention, of course, but this appears to typically involve externally-directed focus. In simple example to safely drive a vehicle it requires a significant amount of focused attention. Also many work activities (as well as reading) require focused attention. On this point I wonder if one of the big contributors to the satisfaction that can come from working simply comes from the requisite focused state.

If you are interested you can find some meditation programs to attend. I recommend trying to find something that is low-key and un-hyped, and don't look for charisma. One of my most memorable experiences as a student was in some classes with a man simply teaching attention. Although highly trained by

Tibetan monastics, his teachings involved simple paying attention exercises. Nothing extra, just the exercises at hand along with his sincere commentary. Enlightenment was not mentioned. Trying to simply pay attention turns out to be very challenging; in its own mundane way enlightening; and of course can be rewarding. Additionally some of the classes I have attended with older Tibetan teachers - which naturally included some religious context - were likewise sincere and involved minimal hype.

Simple introductory practices often involve paying attention to some internal process. This could entail silently counting your breath (on the inhalations, exhalations, or both - up to 10 and then restarting) or just paying attention to your breathing. My first meditation practice involved silently repeating a short word phrase or mantra. The idea is to try to patiently and persistently stay with your meditational focus. Again it is sounds easy, but isn't. Our minds are so inclined towards wondering and our attention is very easily detoured into our established scripts. To facilitate the process it is typically recommended that you sit up relatively straight and have a quiet bland setting. Mostly I just sit on a meditation cushion and stare downward towards an adjacent blank wall. Although performed for years, the basic recurrence of catching my mind wandering and then starting again with a focus continues to this day.

Another kind of meditation involves walking while staying focused on a practice. In this way I regularly pace back and forth in my living room in quiet fashion. Occasionally I might check to feel my legs and feet. When we get locked into our head trips we tend to loose connections elsewhere. You can of course try to integrate the paying attention or a awareness effort into other aspects of your life.

An initial breakthrough aspect is that you can come to vividly realize that the default mind state is self-sustained distraction (i.e., 'blah-blah-blah-me, blah-blah-blah-me, …'). As a result I am regularly amazed when intellectuals express grand views of the mind and thinking. For a relevant illustration consider a trip to a grocery store. When I visit they are invariably playing some kind of background music and this invariably draws some kind of mental reaction. Unless I am trying to pay attention I tend to get unconsciously caught up in responding. If I like the song then I may start quietly singing along or humming. That kind of process I think provides a simple introduction to how our internal distraction can happen. We perceive and then react to external (or sometimes internal) stimuli and this then elicits an orchestra of follow-up, including memories and of course emotions. This default wandering or grasping mind-state, unfortunately can distort our experiences and also the habitual blah-blah-blah-me routine can tend to lock us into our repetitive grooves and insensitivities (and in my case seems to limit my appreciation of music).

By limiting external distractions, sitting meditation allows the underlying mind mechanics to become more apparent and with that we can become a bit wiser to our incessant Talk Radio tendencies. This is a humbling process but it can facilitate some helpful awareness or clarity.

Another basic point here is that I suggest meditators - even experienced ones - not abandon a simple daily focused practice. Maybe for lay practice that is the best way to go. The contemporary trends seem to emphasize unfocused or open meditation but I think that comes at a cost. A simple focus - such as trying to follow your breath or counting your breath (up to 10 and then starting over) - offers a practical exercise in simple awareness. You might think of this as a daily mind calisthenics. The alternative open style, perhaps akin to multitasking, can easily be a distracted experience. I saw recently that the American meditation teacher Adyashanti commented that many of the experienced meditators he was encountering had difficulty simply focusing or concentrating. Without a daily focused practice this can easily happen as I have observed with myself. The development of concentration was in fact a basic part of traditional Buddhist mind training, and that development was viewed as a necessary preliminary for mediation.

Perhaps the ultimate challenge with any meditation practice - or other spiritual practices - is to try to balance the need for focusing (on prayer or mediation) with the complementary need for openness. They are both important aspects of engaged living and their balancing seems like an ongoing vital art.

Moving along to comment on a particular challenge with meditation practice. If you are seriously committed to meditation efforts then you may want to see the book, *After the Ecstasy, the Laundry*, by Jack Kornfeld. That book sheds some light on the fact that with sustained meditation practice there can be significant sub-enlightenment breakthroughs (sometimes termed openings) but that in the subsequent lay realm these can be upended. There really are challenges associated with serious meditation practice which might be consistent with the traditional low-key emphasis on lay meditation.

And for those considering significant sustained meditation it appears to be best to find an experienced person and/or group for some ongoing support and feedback. This likely holds for other spiritual or religious practices too.

Within the current meditation scene it might be a challenge to find some experienced and long-term oriented help. Living a sane everyday life is not easy and it might a good idea to be pleased with whatever help you can get. In addition to my meditation/spiritual practice I also try to get outside regularly. I find that outdoor walks can be therapeutic and also somewhat of a meditative experience.

I add some final meditation commentary. There are some good books attempting to offer some help to people with an interest in meditating. On the other hand there are also not surprisingly plenty of superficial ones too. A common tendency is to sell meditation/enlightenment in an effortless or cliche-deep way. Another unhelpful approach is to pander to science. *Waking Up* has company in that regard. The book by Robert Wright entitled *Why Buddhism is True: The Science and Philosophy of Meditation and Enlightenment* appears to be based on the author's need to make sure that Buddhist meditation is scientifically-kosher. I have to admit to being embarrassed that something that I am involved with is home to so much intellectual wannabe-ism.

One helpful book is Shunryu Suzuki's *Zen Mind, Beginner's Mind*. It is simple but also subtle and was derived from talks given during Zen meditation periods (and "enlightenment" only shows up in passing). Suzuki opened his Prologue with:

> People say that practicing Zen is difficult, but there is a misunderstanding as to why. It is not difficult because it is hard to sit in the cross-legged position, or to attain enlightenment. It is difficult because it is hard to keep your mind pure and our practice pure in its fundamental sense [Suzuki, p.1].

First, his opening two "not difficult" assertions are actually difficult, but perhaps this was done to emphasize the third point. The "cross-legged position" referred to is later identified as being full lotus posture! And I have already mentioned the difficulty of encountering significant enlightenment experiences. But the emphasized latter point is a good one and Suzuki closed his Prologue with an elaboration on what "pure" implies:

> So, the most difficult thing is always to keep your beginner's mind. There is no need to have a deep understanding of Zen. Even though you read much Zen literature, you must read each sentence with a fresh mind. You should not say, "I know what Zen is," or "I have attained enlightenment." This is also the secret of the arts: always be a beginner. Be very, very careful about this point. If you start to practice zazen [Zen meditation], you will begin to appreciate your beginner's mind. It is the secret of Zen practice [pp.2-3].

People at the talks he gave were already doing some meditation (although likely many weren't sitting in full lotus). His point here is that the big picture goal is trying to stay with life closely and attentively, analogous to what a beginner might do. In following any spiritual practice this could be a good idea. His Zen center was a different kind than where the aforementioned Ittetsu Nemoto trained at, it emphasized meditation focused on following the breath and was likely much less intense. Furthermore, I have to wonder if similar centers are still functioning.

Of additional note here is that as Suzuki pointed out, following the breath (or other internal meditation focuses), shouldn't be an be exclusive process. It is a subtle point but he suggested that the purpose of:

> practice is to open your small mind. So concentrating is just an aid to help you realize "big mind", or the mind that is everything. If you want to discover the true meaning of Zen in your everyday life, you have to understand the meaning of keeping your mind on your breathing and your body in the right posture [while meditating] [p.16].

In this commentary if you would like you might generalize (as I'm inclined to) and go beyond "Zen", and some of the associated specifics. Concentrating or focusing in an internal sense - as is present in many religious/spiritual practices - can somehow allow us to perceive in a more steady way our big picture including external challenges. This seems to relate to Lusseyran's point about appreciating "things outside" and "things inside". Finally, although Suzuki's commentary might have been language-limited, it nicely covered aspects of engaged living.

A very insightful book is the aforementioned *I AM THAT* involving a wide range of conversations with an Indian teacher (and store owner) Sri Nisargadatta Maharaj. These took place during meditational and chanting practice sessions. Nisargadatta seems to have plumbed the depths of meditation and with it gotten a close view of our inner psyches and difficulties. Nisargadatta, although without a formal education, also somehow seemed to be remarkably lucid with his descriptions and in his ability to instruct through often challenging responses.

In earlier works, including [Christopher 2020a] and [Christopher 2023, Chapter 7], I gave a sizable exchange with Nisagardatta's take on life's inevitable pain, pleasure, and our default conflicting responses to the two [Nisargadata, p.278]. In short he suggested that we hang in there with both and that the inevitable pain/difficulty can help open the door to unseating, our supervisory egos. His subsequent point was to let that hanging-in-there tendency continue to in fact observe our deeper mental terrain and in that way move towards a fuller understanding and possible liberation. I then followed up that segment with a seeming parallel found in Andrew Solomon's book *Far From the Tree* in which the very inspiring dedication of some parents to their children's difficulties was highlighted. Perhaps we are at best - and our life-learning most effective - when we simply hang in there with our inevitable trying situations. This could also be consistent with the suggestion of the aforementioned, Ittetsu Nemoto, that we tend to learn through suffering.

I move on to consider another basic exchange in *I AM THAT*. "Q" here designates the questioner and "M" designates Nisargadatta (the Maharaj). Here goes:

> Q: Unless I am told what to do and how to do it, I feel lost.
>
> M: By all means do feel lost! As long as you feel competent and confident, reality is beyond your reach. Unless you accept inner adventure as a way of life, discovery will not come to you.

Q: Discovery of what?

M: Of the centre of your being, which is free of all directions, all means and ends.

Q: Be all, know all, have all?

M: Be nothing, know nothing, have nothing. This is the only life worth living, the only happiness worth having.

Q: I may admit that the goal is beyond my comprehension. Let me know my way at least.

M: You must find your own way. Unless you find it yourself it will not be your own way and will take you nowhere. Earnestly live your truth as you have found it - act on the little you have understood. It is earnestness that will take you through, not cleverness - your own or another's [Nisargadatta, p.523].

The suggestion here appears to be that there is something basic and subtle within us that can be uncovered. Remember Lusseyran's characterization that "[a] click suffice[s], a slight change in point of view". And also Suzuki's point to try to stay in beginner-mode and thus with it to facilitate an embrace of life's inherent "inner adventure". That something really isn't supposed to be spectacular (although uncovering it may constitute quite a jolt), or even practical; but it is something vital and meaningful.

I go on here to somewhat contradict the above assertion that "[y]ou must find your own way". There really were practices to follow including at establishments like Nisargadatta's. Somehow those practices were supposed to facilitate what might be termed spiritual progress. In any case, at a later point in *I AM THAT* a description is given of what he thinks needs to ultimately transpire to have a breakthrough experience. A student with some apparent frustration asks Nisargadatta about the demanding meditational practices. Essentially 'what gives with these difficult practices (or sadhanas)?!?!'. And Nisargadatta responded:

> M: Unless you make tremendous efforts, you will not be convinced that effort will take you nowhere. The self is so self-confident, that unless it is totally discouraged, it will not give up. Mere verbal conviction is not enough. Hard facts alone can show the absolute nothingness of the self-image.

My take here is that derailing the immense Me-freight-train, in order to facilitate a deeper life-connection and with it meaning, is a huge project (although the underlying issues may be subtle), and that religions/spiritual traditions have tried to tackle this with various practices. And although such practices seemingly contradict Nisardatta's "[y]ou must find your own way" claim, the prescribed processes and requisite earnestness are supposed to help "take [us] through". Finally, hopefully this process will not take "billions of kalpa" to complete.

The traditional framing of sustained meditational practices is largely within a life-after-life perspective. One finds workable practices so that one can further appreciate the lessons of life, facilitate helping others, and grow some in what could be described as a spiritual/religious or simply hanging-in-there sense. I think traditionally people involved in such practices didn't expect a final breakthrough in the current lifetime and certainly not in an easy fashion. Sages are very rare. From a Buddhist perspective a book like Thondup's *Peaceful Death, Joyful Rebirth* discusses the potential for improvement or even a breakthrough following death. Other religions, of course, have their own post-death suggestions and salvation scenarios.

With some patience and persistence, perhaps we can begin to appreciate the points made by Lusseyran that in fact the really meaningful aspects of life, which he characterized as "light" and "joy", do "not come from outside", they somehow have a home within us.

Chapter 4 - Final Discussions

A basic message in this book is that science's vision of life is far from a certainty. In fact it is easily questioned. There are a numerous clear behavioral challenges as well as an unfolding general problem with DNA's role as the language of life. Something else appears to be going on. When you roll in our innate religious sense then you have a starting point to consider digging into religious/mystical questions.

This book has pointed out some failures encountered in attempting to identify the specific codes behind heritable traits, in particular with regards to our behavioral ones. In a similar vein, the banished scientist Rupert Sheldrake, focused on the need for additional physical factors to explain the origin of the form and functioning of organisms. With regard to this, Sheldrake has the aforementioned bet against a claim made by the biologist Lewis Wolpert [Sheldrake bet]. Wolpert's claim is that:

> [b]y 1 May 2029, given the genome of a fertilized egg of an animal or plant, we will be able to predict in at least one case all the details of the organism that develops from it, including any abnormalities.

After acknowledging the complexity of organisms, Wolpert went on to add that:

> [t]o win the bet, we will have to be able to predict the behavior of almost all the cells in the embryo. In a small worm, say the nematode Caenorhabditis elegans, there are 959 cells, making it the ideal model to solve this problem. It is a major challenge, but

advances in cell biology, systems biology and computing will take us there.

Sheldrake, though, was not buying this and began his response by simply stating "Wolpert's faith in the predictive power of the genome is misplaced". He went on to detail some of the enormous complexity hurdles facing DNA. In the end Sheldrake pointed out that:

> Wolpert is not alone in believing in the predictive value of the genome. Governments, venture capitalists and medical charities have bet and are still betting billions of dollars on it. More than a case of fine port [the wine wager] is at stake.

I greatly appreciate Rupert Sheldrake's efforts and commentary, not least because he sincerely tries to be polite despite his banishment from science. But I disagree with his response. Instead I suggest that:

> there are clear differences in human innate behavioral tendencies and these are supposed to be largely derived from differences in DNA. Given the limited amount of variable DNA that we possess; the existence of clear patterns of heredity; the official genomic expectations; and finally the wide-scale failure of extensive searches thru that variable DNA: it is now reasonable to conclude that the genome accounts for much less of human behavioral variation than was expected. A comparable situation has unfolded with the disease susceptibility expectations of personal genomics. This represents a basic failure of the scientific understanding of life and by implication its evolution.

Given the nature of behavioral challenges - including a big spread in innate intellectual abilities down to very specific behavioral shifts as found with autism, schizophrenia, or transgender phenomena - significant DNA connections should have already been uncovered.

Thus, I am suggesting then that a bet about genome-based predictions for the specifics of a 959 cell worm extending forward 10 years, is too little and too late. The relevant human challenge is found in personal genomics and behavioral genetics. That is where the shortcomings of science's genetics-heredity model are increasingly apparent. We should not simply believe "[b]ecause [science] said so". And there is little need to read the genetics literature. In such literature the relevant findings can be hard to uncover. In popular news relevant synopses tend to be more transparent, and to this day such news might best be titled "The Missing Heritability Continues To Go Missing".

Additionally, as presented in the first chapter there are a number of behavioral phenomena that are very unlikely to be consistent with science's molecular-only model of life. I again suggest that the most significant is our innate religious/dualistic understanding which is suggestive of a number of things. It is consistent with something deeper going on with life; that we (and perhaps animals as well) have had some exposure to it; and that this situation offers some support for religious perspectives.

For those interested in investigating religious and/or spiritual understandings of life, I suggest that the DNA deficit situation should be a significant focus. The behavioral challenges are obviously important too, but the objective and general nature of the missing heritability problem make it stand out. If science's molecular-only model is accurate then how much mystery is really left with regard to life? Certainly some unusual behaviors, surprising outcomes, and of course explaining consciousness. Intellectuals will likely tend to avoid the first two of these, and spend way too much energy on the ambiguous terrain of consciousness. If DNA strikes out, though, it suggests science is wrong about life and evolution. From a religious perspective there could be some unidentified top-down (God or gods) contributions and/or from the complementary bottom-up (souls or spirits) perspective there could be additional ones. Perhaps in a simple way monozygotic twins embody a good chunk of this mystery. In a physical appearance sense they are often almost identical as expected from a materialist perspective (Check). In a deeper way though, beginning with personality they are not (No Check). It would be nice to think that some academics/intellectuals would be interested in investigating this situation, as opposed to engaging in endless nature-plus-nurture doublespeak.

◆ ◆ ◆

I go on now to consider some possible practical ramifications. Beyond the Who-We-Are and What-Happens-To-Us mysteries implied by the missing heritability problem, there might also be practical implications. I remember a serious review of an E. O. Wilson book in *Scientific American* years ago. As is not uncommon in such future-oriented, science-based books, E. O. Wilson's conjured up some optimistic conclusions with regards to humanity's unfolding sustainability and eco-management crises. The reviewer was also a biologist and they rejected this optimism. That reviewer concluded humans will not make significant sacrifices for future generations. Given science's materialist, this-life-only, selfish-inclined vision of humans, the reviewer's conclusions were reasonable. Deeper investigations of human beings (and animals) might, though find support for different views on this situation. With a sequential life or reincarnation model, in which souls tend to cycle thru lives, the existential logic could be shifted.

Somewhat consistent with this, in Michael Tobias' searing man-versus-nature epic, *World War III*, the group identified for their encouraging sustainability and ecological priorities were the lay Jains. Their religion, Jainism, presents a world view of souls cycling thru lives and a belief in the sanctity of all those souls. Souls are even posited for plants. In any case a very high priority for Jains is to minimize the suffering imposed on other souls (which can lead to apparent excess among the monks and also some complicated ethical logic, though). Their ultimate religious goal is to achieve freedom from reincarnation and the associated ignorance. This is believed to be a huge task as can be gleaned from a synopsis [Jainworld]. Paired with that personal goal is one of assisting other beings in doing the same. In any case, Tobias' discussion suggests that Jains tend to have a good disposition towards ecological challenges.

In his 2018 book, *Enlightenment Now*, Pinker praised the trends in the modern world. I very briefly return here to some previous writings in which I questioned at some length his optimism [Christopher 2020b]. One official reviewer, Ian Goldin, an economist and professor of Globalization and Development at Oxford has authored books that overlap some with *Enlightenment Now*'s scope [Goldin]. Golden wrote in a *Nature* review that "[e]conomic growth has come at the expense of ecosystems" and that:

> Pinker does cite climate change, but as a worrying exception to a relentlessly positive narrative, rather than as the most glaring example of a wider failure of global commons management.

One might then criticize Pinker's mostly singular focus on global warming by considering the gross makeover humanity has carried out on the biosphere. Golding also pointed out some stubborn obstacles to good decision-making in the form of what might be termed culture.

I further consider some ecological challenges that appeared to have been shortchanged in *Enlightenment Now*. For a big picture sense, readers might look at works such as "The biomass distribution on Earth" by Yinon M. Bar-On, Rob Phillips, and Ron Milo [Bar-On *et al* 2018] and also Vaclav Smil's "Harvesting the Biosphere" article (or book by the same name) [Smil 2015a]. Such big comprehensive works are necessarily complicated in having to make difficult estimates of historical quantities (including those for tiny lifeforms). Nonetheless, they represent very significant studies. In Bar-On *et al* they presented estimates that "the mass of humans is [about] an order of magnitude [10x] higher than that of all wild mammals combined". They also pointed out that our modern innovations have facilitated growth in our population that "have had radical ecological effects". They wrote that total mass of domesticated birds (primarily chickens) is now about three times that of wild birds. Arguments about our purported "Enlightened" status should include a look at our ecological shadow which has grown markedly during the modern era.

Bar-On *et al* also cited the work of Barnosky which suggested that the contemporary total weight of wild mammals (both terrestrial and marine) is about one-sixth that of their pre-human exposure level. But by adding in the mass of humans and our livestock, though, that loss goes from a factor of six to a gain of about a factor of four.

Pinker was also generally critical of the ecological inclinations of indigenous or premodern people. He states that as humans get better educated and richer, they tend to care more about the environment and are more active in trying to preserve it. He also wrote that:

> [w]hen native peoples first step foot in an ecosystem, they typically hunted large animals to extinction, and often cleared vast swaths of forest. A dirty secret of the conservation movement is that wilderness preserves are set up only after indigenous peoples have been decimated or forcibly removed from them, including the national parks of United States and the Serengeti in East Africa [Pinker 2018, p.123].

Pinker might have tried to quantify this and might have offered a bar graph roughly describing the gross historical decline of nature and/or biodiversity. On the left could have been bars representing the decline before the Enlightenment period and on the right bars showing the subsequent decline. I believe that such a bar graph would have contradicted Pinker's point.

Some relevant articles were found in the April and May 2020 issues of *Scientific American* and they dealt with traditional cultures and their very difficult transitions into the modern realm. The first of these was April's "The Aid Tsunami: How disaster relief ravaged an indigenous community" by Ajay Saini and Simron J. Singh [Saini and Singh]. A healthy island-based traditional community, the Nicobarese, had their lives upended by the 2004 Indian Ocean tsunami. This situation was then furthered as their way of life was overrun by an intervention of modern charity (essentially a second long-lived tsunami). The second troubling tale was May's, "Living With the Forest: [BaYaka] Pygmies thrived in the Congo Basin - until development coupled with conservation arrived" by Jerome Lewis [Lewis]. Another story of traditional ways and the ensuing terrible derailment encountered in the modern world.

A significant commonality in these stories was that both traditional cultures appear to have been bolstered by their particular spiritual or religious beliefs. The authors of both articles had lived with their respective subjects prior to their disruptions and seem to have come to really appreciate their intertwined spiritual and nature-oriented ways. It is noteworthy that some traditional lifestyles have existed for long periods in relative harmony with nature.

The fact that such lifestyles also appeared to maintain a good quality of human wellbeing is obviously significant too. Both articles are outstanding and as such recommended reading, but for brevity here I go a little further with the pygmy report. In that article the author Jerome Lewis wrote that "BaYaka hold that the forest is abundant so long as everyone respects certain principles". Those principles involving sharing and also land management were briefly given. The BaYaka pygmies believe that the "forest cares about its inhabitants and desirers to hear delightful sounds emanating from them; sharing song and laughter with it will induce it to be munificent". Lewis then claimed that "the key social institutions of the BaYaka not only ensure abundance but also celebrate and generate joy." Lewis claimed that his family's experience with the Bayaka in the 1990's had been "idyllic", a time in which they "ate wild foods and moved freely without fear" and had partaken in extensive "spirit plays".

Jerome Lewis also felt his family's time with the BaYaka pygmies was somewhat consistent with the conclusions of anthropologist Colin Turnbull about his experiences with the BaMbuti Pygmies three decades earlier (and 1,000 kilometers away). Turnbull had then written:

> [T]hey were a people who had found in the forest something that made their life more than just worth living, something that made it, with all of its hardships and problems and tragedies, a wonderful thing full of happiness and free of care.

Perhaps some premodern people found their own enlightenments/Enlightenments. This might be of interest to some modern people. Furthermore, perhaps spreading our modern Enlightened ways can ultimately be harmful to some people.

Also noteworthy herein is that these thoroughly non-modern people somehow found their own religious truths and trajectories. Despite being outside any of the established big religions they seem to have found stable deep spiritual connections. Perhaps this demonstrates that with sufficient commitment or earnestness we can all find our spiritual ways.

Finally, in a positive turn and in contrast to Pinker's claims, the article pointed out that "[r]esearchers, activists and others from mainstream society are recognizing that local communities are the primary protectors of nature and are seeking to help them". I wish them luck with their efforts.

I add some personal observations on these practical matters. In the past I used to eat lunch with a highly educated, nonreligious person. That person was clear about the threat associated with climate change but they had minimal concern about it. On this point they said simply, 'I'll be gone before it gets serious'. That person for further context was a long time participant in secularized (Western) Buddhism and they also had a part-time connection to the nuclear power industry (a significant and promising energy option touted by Pinker). This person seemed to very good credentials to be considered Enlightened in a Western sense, and was also in pursuit of the spiritual goals of secular Buddhism. And yet that person had minimal concern about climate change and thus their perspective seemed consistent with the conclusions of the earlier mentioned biologist book reviewer. Furthermore I add that as a relatively educated person who has spent plenty of time around other relatively educated and nominally Enlightened people, I have to say I am not optimistic that the Enlightened or intellectual perspective is adequate to meeting the demands of our unfolding ecological/sustainability challenges.

A basic point raised by Steven Pinker in *Enlightenment Now* is about the supposedly progressive/helpful inclinations of contemporary and increasingly secular people. In fact if that were true - beyond the kind of trendy intellectualisms and posturing many of us modern-ers partake in - then I suggest we would not be where we are in our sustainability showdown.

◆ ◆ ◆

I move on to consider the two big areas of pure science. The first area is biology and here materialism is obviously a fixture. The other is physics and materialism is apparently even more of a fixture there. Mark Gober in his *The End of Upside Down Thinking* gave some samples of the contempt for paranormal reports found among physicists [Gober, pp.195-8]. I add that when your research area is highly speculative and incredibly remote you are probably not inclined to want to hear about everyday jaw-dropping psychic phenomena or more generally other behavioral conundrums. Furthering the situation is that physics has created for itself a largely unquestioned role as the final authority on objective reality. Analogously, going forward neuroscience is likely to be taken as the official interpreter of subjective reality.

I go on here to approach contemporary physics in a roundabout way. As a kid for a while I really enjoyed reading about amazing feats such as those chronicled in *Ripley's Believe it or Not!* and the *Guinness Book of World Records*. After a few years, though, I came to see the process as mostly empty. I would get a short term cerebral 'Wow!' thinking about some bizarre feats, but it didn't change anything for me or likely the participants. Years later as an adult I saw an article about a graduating college senior who was gushing about her plans to study the 'philosophical implications of quantum mechanics'. Something then clicked as it dawned on me that a good deal of the attention on modern physics could really be an analogous 'Wow! Think of that!'-phenomena. Somewhat overlapping with this might be the near worship-like following generated by the presumed brilliance of physicists.

My previous books looked critically at Sean Carroll's dismissal of paranormal phenomena and also support for a Many Worlds interpretation for quantum mysteries [Carroll 2016; 2019]. Here I consider Kaku's *The God Equation*, which not unlike other books by physicists appears to draw a serious readership and even some religion-related interest. Kaku's primary mission (and he has plenty of company) is to finally nail down a very complicated physical explanation for the universe and in particular, its dynamics. He hopes to accomplish this with a "1 inch equation".

For his introduction to the historical contributions of physics consider:

> [w]e have seen how the mastery of the four fundamental forces has not only revealed many of the secrets of nature but has also unleashed the great

scientific revolutions that have altered the destiny of civilization itself. When Newton wrote down the laws of motion and gravity, he laid the groundwork for the Industrial Revolution. When Faraday and Maxwell revealed the unity of the electric and magnetic force, this set into motion the electric revolution [Kaku, p.182].

Kaku went on to suggest that Einstein and quantum researchers then initiated the "high-tech revolution of today" [p.182]. Kaku appeared to neglect that this whole process of physics-bounded thinking has shortchanged questions surrounding life and with it meaning (although he did go as far as to suggest that a "purely mathematical term in an equation from physics" cannot explain "love or happiness"). He also appeared to neglect the sober side-effects of our physical progress. Kaku appears to share Pinker's optimism about our modern trajectory.

In the closing sections of *The God Equation* Kaku tried to inject some meaning associated with the pursuits of contemporary physics. He did, though, write with regard to the impact of finding the equation of his book's title, that "as far as a direct impact on our lives, it probably will be minimal" [p.183]. His earlier depictions had effectively carved out a super-sized role for physicists with regard to technical developments. This even included a small chapter which concluded that our understanding of life was now "the product of quantum mechanics" [p.87]. It is notable that the overall impressive, nature-kosher lives and insights of some traditional groups like the pygmies, apparently were accomplished without science, let alone quantum mechanics.

Kaku goes beyond his initial humbling conclusion to add a bit. He pointed out that "that the bedrock of our understanding of the world is science, which is ultimately based on things that are testable, reproducible, [and] falsifiable" [p.189]. One might counter this, though, by pointing out that much of our personal understanding comes through direct observation and experience. Furthermore, a good chunk of our experiences do not appear to be reproducible, and I suggest that a good part of our frustrations tends to come from assuming otherwise.

Kaku also offered along the way quotes to the effect that physics has been home to the "world's greatest thinkers" and the world's "greatest intellectual debate". Consistent with this he also provided samples of the corresponding overreach of physics. Consider:

> Thus, the multiverse idea allows one to combine the creation mythology of Christianity with the Nirvana of Buddhism into a single theory that is compatible with known physical laws [p.194].

And in a Stephen Hawking's quote:

> If we do discover a complete theory, it should in time be understandable in broad principle by everyone, not just a few scientists. Then we shall, philosophers, scientists, and just ordinary people, be able to take part in the discussion of the question of why it is that we and the universe exist. If we find the answer to that, it would be the ultimate triumph of human reason - for then we would know the mind of God [p.198].

It is worth noting problems here with Hawking's reasoning. There is no reason for a complete theory to address the "question of why it is that we" "exist". Do any physicists (including the late Hawking) question materialism? From that perspective you inevitably have to wheel in luck in a prominent role as to how homo sapiens came about, and then further at the individual level to deliver any person's presumed individual-defining DNA blueprint. On the latter point, remember how lucky you presumably are to be alive given your dependence on a very unlikely conception that produced your particular DNA blueprint, which as Richard Dawkins put it, "created [you], body and mind" [Dawkins, p.20].

Finally, Kaku himself offered a conclusion on the ultimate implications of a God (or Theory of Everything) Equation:

> But one day, perhaps facing the death of our universe, our descendants may be able to use their formidable scientific know-how to channel enough positive energy to open a tunnel through space and time, and then use negative energy (from the Casimir effect) to stabilize the gateway. One day, our descendants will master the Planck energy, the energy at which space and time become unstable, and use their powerful technology to escape our dying universe.
>
> In this way, quantum gravity, instead of being an exercise in the mathematics of eleven-dimensional space-time, becomes a cosmic inter-dimensional lifeboat allowing intelligent life to evade the second law of thermodynamics and escape to a much warmer universe.
>
> So the theory of everything is more than just a beautiful mathematical theory. Ultimately, it could be our only salvation [Kaku, p.196].

Another physics-framed example came in a *Scientific American* article by Caleb Scharf, "The Benevolence of Black Holes" [Scharf]. In it Scharf laid out some evidence of the apparent dynamic existing between the structure of a galaxy and its central black hole, and ultimately for the resulting potential to support the development of life. Scharf pointed out that:

> The connection between the phenomenon of life and the size and activity of supermassive black holes is

quite simple. A fertile and temperate galactic zone is far more likely to occur in the type of galaxy that contains a modestly large, regularly nibbling, black hole rather than a voracious but long since spent monster.

Scharf went on to report that our Milky Way galaxy happens to be "smack dab in the [life-habitable] sweet spot of supermassive black hole activity". Furthermore, Scharf wrote that:

> [t]he entire chain of events leading to you and me would be different or even nonexistent without the coevolution of galaxies with supermassive black holes and the extraordinary [matter and energy] regulation they perform.

The details then of the universe's galaxies appear to have been dependent on black hole dynamics and this would seem to add to the already huge evolution- and conception-based odds against the existence of "you and me".

Scharf's black hole article opened with:

> [o]ur existence in this place, this microscopic corner of the cosmos, is fleeting. With utter disregard for our wants and needs, nature plays out its grand acts on scales of space and time that are truly hard to grasp. Perhaps all that we can look to for real solace is our endless capacity to ask questions and seek answers about the place we find ourselves in.

And it concluded in reverential fashion:

> This fertile corner of the cosmos has been governed by all that has gone on around it, including the behavior of the black hole at our galactic center. The very places that have sealed themselves away from the rest of the universe have served as one of the most

influential forces shaping it. We owe so much to them.

And thus it would seem that we are again intellectually cleared to attempt to find meaning in following the very speculative details of investigations into unimaginably distant, lifeless phenomena. Furthermore, "meaning" here might best be officially characterized via patterns of neural firings.

The materialist perspective (which falls out of the physics-only view of reality) obviously leaves potential purviews of life and meaning in rather stark terms. I suggest that perspective has been increasingly accepted and that further it has contributed to the prevalent escapism found in modern societies. But staying consistent with physics, though, it is worth pointing that most of the universe is missing. Those missing aspects, the previously introduced dark matter and dark energy, appear to account for something like 95 percent of the inferable universe (and subsequent inferences could add more). That official void in our physical understanding of the universe could be home to some of the deeper or spiritual aspects of life, which might in turn have something to do with the universe's physical dynamics. Together these could perhaps offer more promising opportunities for intellectual solace than asking questions about black holes.

A further note here is that if some readers don't care about possible connections to physics that is certainly reasonable. Personally I think life's mysteries are valid in and of themselves (and have quit expecting academic acknowledgment on this point), but note that even with the possible overlap with physics' dark terrain it is unlikely that any physical measurements and/or theories could prove helpful with life's psychological and spiritual challenges.

There is one somewhat subtle point, though, that I make on the subject of possible overlaps between spiritual phenomena and the material universe. Much of the latter might be thoroughly characterizable by equations. That is in a local example, Earth's weather dynamics might be completely describable via equations (some statistical and of course requiring tons of measurements). With life, though, as far as I can see any deeper/religious perspective has to include souls as well as their free will. That freedom would seem to imply a break from equations. All equations, including the hyped ones associated with quantum phenomena, ultimately imply determinism (including those involving statistics). As such they would work against free will. Thus an alternative title for this book could have been *The End of Equations*. It might have been more technically accurate, but also unnecessarily esoteric.

On a final point in this physics-related detour I turn to a quote that showed up on the back cover of a children's book on religion. That book, *How the World Works: Religion* by John Hawkins, I had given to a 12 year old who had expressed an interest in religions. When I stopped by I found amidst their messy room that book backside up. On that back cover there was a quote from the Hindu text, Rig Veda (Chapter 10, Hymn 190) written on it:

> The material creation is only one quarter of the entire cosmos. The eternal spiritual sky is much larger, making up the remaining three-quarters.

Perhaps long ago people not only found some success in making some intimate subjective sense out of life's mysteries, they might also have found a bit of success in characterizing their objective counterparts.

Before giving a few final suggestions on religious or spiritual practices, I insert a few ideas with regard to our initial spiritual dynamic. Earlier in a quote it was suggested that young children have "not yet forgotten or grown confused and distracted by the world" and thus in this interpretation display overt dualistic beliefs (i.e., our innate natural religion) as apparent carryover from pre-birth experiences (which were either part of a sequential life or one-time only trajectory) [Barrett, p.2]. I think there is other evidence consistent with this possible dynamic. As a young child I regularly had dreams of flying around. Essentially disembodied free flight. When I checked about this I saw this is not unusual and perhaps not surprisingly there are many psychological interpretations. The big question with this, though, appears to be how could someone have a vivid dream of something they hadn't experienced. A simple dualistic explanation could follow from earlier pre-birth disembodied experiences. Potentially then before merging with a mother (and with this a future embodied life), a soul might spend time in disembodied flight.

Further, the ending of this early "not yet ... confused" stage could be sort of discrete. Around I think the age of six I can vividly remember lying in bed and having a sense of dread as the sense of my body-based mortality sunk in. Perhaps then when our identification with the body reaches a critical mass that could complete a transition to the subsequent "confused and distracted by the world" state (in which we worry about many things including our bodies and death). I suggest something else might happen as part of this transition to a fixation on embodiment. That is a push to remove our earlier memories of our infant and pre-infant dualistic/religious state. Such a removal could be consistent with the mysterious infant amnesia in which we lose memories of the first 3 or 4 years of our experiences [Lobue; Tucker 2005: p.90]. Thus the soul might be seen as having pushed to eliminate confusing memories from a very different pre-birth and shortly after birth scenario (that of the spirit-oriented realm, if you will). In a somewhat analogous point, the terminal lucidity dynamic might be viewed as also having been initiated by the soul, in that case not to chuck-off memories from a different realm, but in making a determined effort simply for a final shoutout. There may of course be a number of other dynamics explainable in terms of a soul, including perhaps broadly to account for the not infrequent weirdness of dreams and also when we somehow muster extraordinary courage [Dunne; and in a gross sense much of the book, *And There Was Light*].

I move on to conclude with a few comments for those interested in a religious/spiritual practice, whether it be to try one or simply to re-examine an existing practice. Most of my practices are connected with Mahayana Buddhism. Some of these teachings and practices are quite complex, but I find the simple ones more reasonable. Given our seemingly ever increasing options, I find that simplicity is a good consideration.

There appear to be two aspects of a religious or spiritual practice. One is short term potential, which perhaps is bigger in the contemporary scene. The other is long term and this usually includes a post-death horizon. In some of my other works continuity across lives in the form of reincarnation is argued to offer some explanations, and those works also pointed out that there is indirect support for God and souls via their presence as innate beliefs. My experience has been that a long term religious view including faith makes sense and can also be helpful. It seems to have boosted my motivation to find good things to do, and also to simply pay attention which is essential in learning life's lessons.

Continuing, religious theologies can be very involved (although seemingly less so than some medium-based reports or eleven-dimensional space-time, inter-dimensional lifeboats). It might be worth remembering what the thoughtful, one-time-physicist, David Bohm suggested in that 'all descriptions are incomplete '[Bohm and Peat]. Also even if we encountered a complete description how could we possibly digest it? A simpler alternative is that there is something basic and psychological to uncover (or get), and that with it a deeper (or potentially sacred) perspective on life and meaning are revealed. I think *And There Was Light* might be exhibit A for this option. From a this-life-only perspective this kind of breakthrough is apparently difficult to realize, though, but perhaps such breakthroughs are more likely after death as suggested by a number of religions.

The underlying optimism found in a wide-ranging book like *I AM THAT* is that once on board with an inner search we eventually get it. A related point suggested therein is that this inevitable realization would follow from the underlying soul's (or ultimate Self's) determined efforts to break free from life's confusion.

My sense is that if I can stay with the basics - day in and day out - then that should be helpful come what may. Both of the premodern groups considered earlier in this chapter seemed to have found their own religious/spiritual support packages. Perhaps if you are a modern religious person then you can learn a little about some other religious routes and also of course appreciate the fact there are many different spiritual routes practiced.

A critical point worth noting is that the science and intellect-led Enlightenment that Pinker (and others) tout has ultimately had the significant side-effects including diminishing the credibility of religious perspectives. I suggest that science currently plays the lead role in diminishing such alternative views, but that historically generic arrogance has played a big role. Good old fashioned group think - including of course religion-based ones - has led its members to assume the superiority of their views.

Life entails many mysteries and plenty of hidden meaning, perhaps at best we can persevere, try to live ethically, pay attention, and find some support from religious or spiritual traditions.

About the Author

Ted Christopher lives in Rochester, New York. He has held a variety of jobs including some academic-based, biomedical ultrasound efforts. Post-high school, his formal education has been mostly technical and included a PhD in Electrical Engineering. Concurrent with these efforts he has tried to make sense of some basic aspects of life, perhaps influenced by his involvement with Buddhist practices and more generally his religious instincts.

Acknowledgments

The author gratefully acknowledges the Central Library of Rochester and Monroe County. A number of relevant books were obtained at that library. Central Library also offered a good reading and writing space. The author also acknowledges the works of many others who have tried to make sense of life's mysteries.

References

Allegrini A. G., Selzam S., Rimfeld K., von Stumm S., Pingault J. B., and Plomin R. Genomic prediction of cognitive traits in childhood and adolescence. *Molecular Psychiatry*, April 11, 2019. Available at https://www.biorxiv.org/content/10.1101/418210v1 . Accessed on April 18, 2023.

Almaas A. H. *Essence With The Elixir of Enlightenment: The Diamond Approach to Inner Realization*. Newburyport, MA: Weiser Books, 1998.

Austin J. *Zen and the Brain: Toward an Understanding of Meditation and Consciousness*. Cambridge, MA: The MIT Press; 1998. An 844 page effort, so much for the Zen tendency towards minimization.

Balter M. Schizophrenia's Unyielding Mysteries. *Scientific American*, May 2017.

Barnes J. *Nothing to be Frighten of*. New York, NY: Alfred A. Knopf; 2008.

Bar-On Y. M., Phillips R., and Milo R. The biomass distribution on Earth. Available online at www.pnas.org/cgi/doi/10.1073/pnas.1711842115 . Accessed on April 18, 2023.

Barrett J. L. *Born Believers - The Science of Children's Religious Belief*. New York, NY: Free Press; 2012.

Barry E. The 'Nation's Psychiatrist' Takes Stock, With Frustration. *New York Times*, February 22, 2022.

Berg J. J., Harpak A., Sinnott-Armstrong N., Joergensen A. M., Mostafavi H., Field Y., Boyle E. A., Zhang X., Racimo F., Pritchard J. K., and Coop G. Reduced signal for polygenic adaptation of height in UK Biobank. *eLife*, March 21, 2019. Available at https://elifesciences.org/articles/39725 . Accessed on April 18, 2023.

Bering J. One Last Goodbye: The Strange Case of Terminal Lucidity. *Scientific American* Blog entry November 2014. https://blogs.scientificamerican.com/bering-in-mind/one-last-goodbye-the-strange-case-of-terminal-lucidity/ Accessed on April 18, 2023.

Blofeld J. *Zen Teachings of Huang Po*. New York, NY: Grove Press; 1994.

Bohm D. and Peat F. D. *Science, Order, and Creativity: A Dramatic New Look at the Creative Roots of Science and Life*. New York, NY: Bantam; 1987.

Bouchard T. J., Lykken D. T., McGue M., Segal N. L., and Tellegen A. Sources of Human Psychological Differences: The Minnesota Study of Twins Reared Apart. *Science, 250*, October 12, 1990. Online at https://www.researchgate.net/publication/20936587_Sources_of_Human_Psychological_Differences_The_Minnesota_Study_of_Twins_Reared_Apart. Accessed on April 18, 2023.

Bullock P. Many Genes Influence Same-Sex Sexuality, Not a Single 'Gay Gene'. *New York Times*, August 29, 2019.

Burnett III Z. Terminal Lucidity: The Researchers Attempting to Prove Your Mind Lives On Even After You Die. 2018 Available at https://medium.com/mel-magazine/terminal-lucidity-the-researchers-attempting-to-prove-that-your-mind-lives-on-even-after-you-die-385ac1f93dca . Accesed on April 18, 2023.

Burpo T. *Heaven is for Real*. Nashville, TN: Thomas Nelson; 2010.

Buswell R. E., Jr. and Lopez D. S., Jr. 2014. www.tricycle.com/blog/10-misconceptions-about-buddhism . Accessed on April 18, 2023.

Campbell T. C. and Campbell T. M. *The China Study*. Dallas, TX: Benbella Books; 2004.

Carey B. Can We Really Inherit Trauma? *New York Times*, December 10, 2018.

Carroll S. 2016. *The Big Picture: On the Origins of Life, Meaning, and the Universe Itself*. New York, NY: Dutton.

Carroll S. 2019. *Something Deeply Hidden: Quantum Worlds and the Emergence of Spacetime*. New York, NY: Dutton.

Carroll S. His online blog at http://www.preposterousuniverse.com/blog/ . There his gist of reality is succinctly stated in the upper right hand corner. Accessed on April 20, 2023.

Carter C. *Science and the Afterlife Experience*. Rochester, VT: Inner Traditions; 2012.

Catania K. C. Attack of the Zombie Maker. *Scientific American*, February 2021.

Cepelewicz J. New Turmoil Over Predicting the Effects of Genes. *Quantamagazine: Genomics*. April 23, 2019. Available at https://www.quantamagazine.org/new-turmoil-over-predicting-the-effects-of-genes-20190423/ . Accessed on April 18, 2023.

Christopher T. 2017a. Science's Big Problem, Reincarnation's Big Potential, and Buddhists' Profound Embarrassment. Available online at http://www.mdpi.com/2077-1444/8/8/155 . Accessed on April 18, 2023.

Christopher T. 2017b. *A Hole in Science: An Opening for an Alternative Understanding of Life (Expanded Third Edition)*. Available at a number of online book retailers.

Christopher T. 2020a. Religion versus Science II: Why Science Is Wrong about Life and Evolution, and Where Religious Beliefs Can Find Objective Traction. Available online at http://www.mdpi.com/2077-1444/11/10/495 (accessed on April 18, 2022).

Christopher T. 2020b. *Why Science Is Wrong About Life And Evolution: "The Invisible Gene" And Other Essays On Scientism*. Self-published and available at Amazon and other online outlets.

Christopher T. 2022a. Questionable All Along, DNA's Inheritance Role is Now Failing in a Big Way - Does Anyone Care? *Open Journal of Philosophy*. Available online at https://www.scirp.org/journal/paperinformation.aspx?paperid=115120 . Accessed on April 18, 2023. Choose "download" to get the paper properly formatted.

Christopher T. 2022b. Reincarnation as a Complement to the Flawed DNA-Based Model of Life: Potential Contributions to Our Disposition Towards Family and Religion/Spirituality. *Open Journal of Philosophy*. Available online at https://www.scirp.org/journal/paperinformation.aspx?paperid=119098 Accessed on April 18, 2023. Choose "download" to get the paper properly formatted.

Christopher T. 2022c. Meaning beyond Molecules and Hubris: A Gross Case Supporting the General Religious Belief Package and Some Critical Perspectives. *Open Journal of Philosophy*. Available online at https://www.scirp.org/journal/paperinformation.aspx?paperid=121211 Accessed on April 18, 2023. Choose "download" to get the paper properly formatted.

Christopher T. 2022d. Dualism 101: Terminal Lucidity and an Explanation. *Open Journal of Philosophy*. Available online at https://www.scirp.org/journal/paperinformation.aspx?paperid=121479 Accessed on April 18, 2023. Choose "download" to get the paper properly formatted.

Christopher T. 2023. *Meaning Beyond Molecules and Hubris: Religions Are onto Something with Regard to Life and Evolution.* USA: Scientific Research Publishing. Available at a number of online book retailers.

Collins F. *The Language of Life: DNA and the Revolution in Personalized Medicine.* New York, NY: HarperCollins; 2010.

Croston R., Branch C. L., Kozlovsky D. Y., Dukas R., and Pravosudov V. V. Heritability and Evolution of Cognitive Traits. *Behavioral Ecology*, 26(6), 1147-1459, 2015.

Cummins G. *The Road to Immortality.* Surrey, UK: White Crow Books; 2012.

Dawkins R. *The Selfish Gene.* New York, NY: Oxford University Press; 1976.

Dennett D. C. *From Bacteria to Bach: The Evolution of Minds.* New York, NY: W.W. Norton and Company; 2018.

Dunne G. How My Father Taught Me to Be a Man. Wall Street Journal, June 14, 2024.

Fintushel E. Something to Offer. *Tricycle* Fall 2008. Available online at https://tricycle.org/magazine/something-offer/. Accessed on April 18 2023.

Fremantle F. and Trungpa C. *The Tibetan Book of the Dead* (pocket version). Boston, MA: Shambhala Publications; 1992.

Fromme P. and Spence J. C. H. Split Second Reactions. *Scientific American*, May 2017.

Gober M. *An End to Upside Down Thinking*. Cardiff-by-the-Sea, CA: Waterside Press; 2018.

Goldin I. Testing Times for Optimism. *Nature* vol. 554, February 22, 2018.

Godfrey A. 'The Clouds Cleared': what terminal lucidity teaches us about life, death, and dementia. *The Guardian*, February 23, 2021. Available online at https://www.theguardian.com/society/2021/feb/23/the-clouds-cleared-what-terminal-lucidity-teaches-us-about-life-death-and-dementia. Accessed on April 18, 2023.

Goodenough U. *The Sacred Depths of Nature*. New York, NY: Oxford University Press; 1998.

Green E. D. Human Genome, Then and Now. *New York Times*, April 15, 2013.

Hall S. S. Revolution Postponed. *Scientific American*, October 2010.

Harris J. R. *No Two Alike*. New York, NY: W. W. Norton & Company; 2006.

Harris S. *Waking Up*. New York, NY: Simon & Schuster; 2014.

Herron J. C. and Freeman S. et al. *Evolutionary Analysis, Fifth Edition*. Pearson Education; 2014.

Holden J. M., EdD, Greyson B., MD, and James D., MSN, RN. *The Handbook of Near-Death Experiences*. Santa Barbara, CA: Praeger Publishers; 2009.

Hopkins W. D., Russell J. L., and Schaefer J. Chimpanzee intelligence is heritable. *Current Biology*, 24:1649-1652, 2014.

Horgan J. blogs.scientificamerican.com/cross-check/2014/10/14/quest-for-intelligence-genes-churns-out-more-dubious-results/ Accessed on April 20, 2023.

Hossenfelder S. and McGaugh S. S. Is Dark Matter Real? *Scientific American*, August 2018.

IPBES Global Assessment Summary for Policymakers. Available online at https://ipbes.net/news/ipbes-global-assessment-summary-policymakers-pdf . Accessed on April 18, 2023.

Jacobs G. H. and Nathans J. The Evolution of Primate Color Vision. *Scientific American*, April 2009.

Jainworld. Spiritual Progress (Gunashtan). Available online at https://jainworld.com/philosophy/spiritual-progress-gunashtan/ . Accessed on April 18, 2023.

Kaku M. *The God Equation: The Quest for a Theory of Everything*. New York, NY: First Anchor Books; 2021.

Kapleau P. *Three Pillars of Zen*. Garden City, NY: Anchor Books; 1980.

Kingsley D. M. From Atoms to Traits. *Scientific American*, January 2009.

Kolata G. Live Long? Die Young? Answer Isn't Just in Genes. *New York Times*, August 31, 2006.

Kosik S. K. *The Way Forward*. *Scientific American*, May 2020. Also note additional articles in this issue.

Landau E. Born in male body, Jenny knew early that she was a girl. CNN, June 14, 2009. Available at www.cnn.com/2009/HEALTH/06/12/sex.change.gender.transition/ . Accessed on April 18, 2023.

Latham J. and Wilson A. The Great DNA Data Deficit: Are Genes for Disease a Mirage? Available at https://www.independentsciencenews.org/health/the-great-dna-data-deficit/. Accessed on April 18, 2023.

Lee J. J., and 79 more authors/contributors. Gene discovery and polygenic prediction from a 1.1 million-person GWAS of educational attainment. *Nature Genetics* 50, 2018, pp. 1112-1121. Available at https://scholar.harvard.edu/files/laibson/files/ssgac_nature-genetics_072318.pdf . Accessed on April 18, 2023.

Leister M. B. Personality changes following heart transplantation: The role of cellular memory. *Medical Hypothesis*, 2020, v.135, February.

Lello L., Avery S. G., Tellier L., Vazquez A. I., de los Campos G., and Hsu S. D. H. Accurate Genomic Prediction of Human Height. *Genetics* Vol. 210, pp.477-97. Available online at https://www.genetics.org/content/210/2/477. Accessed on April 18, 2023.

Lester R. J. A New Therapy for Multiple Personality Disorder Helps a Woman with 12 Selves. *Scientific American*, June 2023.

Levine N. *The Miraculous 16th Karma*. Merigar, Italy; Shang Shung Publications; 2013.

Lewin R. Is Your Brain Really Necessary? *Science*, Vol. 210, December 12, 1980. Available at www.rifters.com/real/articles/Science_No-Brain.pdf. Accessed on April 18, 2023.

Lewis J. Living With the Forest: Pygmies Thrived in the Congo Basin - Until Development Coupled with Conservation Arrived. *Scientific American*, May 2020.

Lightman A. *The Transcendent Brain: Spirituality in the Age of Science*. New York, NY: Pantheon Books; 2023.

Luhrmann T. M. 2012. Beyond the Brain. *The Wilson Quarterly*, Summer 2012:28-34.

Luhrmann T. M. 2020. *How God Becomes Real*. Princeton, NJ: Princeton University Press.

Lunde D. T. Psychiatric complications of heart transplants. *Am. J. Psychiatry*, 1967, 124, 1190-1195.

Lusseyran J. *And There Was Light*. Novato, CA: New World Library; 2014.

MacFarquhar L. Last Call. *The New Yorker*, June 24, 2013. Available online at www.newyorker.com/magazine/2013/06/24/last-call-3. Accessed on April 18, 2023.

Matthiessen P. *Nine-Headed Dragon River: Zen Journals 1969-1982*. Boulder, CO: Shambhala Publications; 1998.

Mayer E. L. *Extraordinary Knowing: Science, Skepticism, and the Inexplicable Powers of the Human Mind*. New York, NY: Bantom Books; 2007.

Mayer G. Book review: Dean Radin: Supernormal: Science, Yoga, and the Evidence for Extraordinary Psychic Abilities. Originally in *Journal of Scientific Explorations*, 28(2):403-408, June 2013.

Mayr E. *What Evolution Is*. New York, NY: Basic Books; 2001.

McCarthy M. Mukherjee follows cancer best seller with 'The Gene'. Available online at https://www.usatoday.com/story/life/books/2016/05/19/the-gene-an-intimate-history-siddhartha-mukherjee-book-review/84201180/ Accessed on April 18, 2023.

McGaugh J. L. and LePort A. Remembrance of All Things Past. *Scientific American*, February 2014.

Mendoza M. A. Terminal Lucidity Revisited. *Psychology Today*, September 30, 2019. Available online at https://www.psychologytoday.com/us/blog/understanding-grief/201909/terminal-lucidity-revisited . Accessed on April 18, 2023.

Meyer S. C. *Darwin's Doubt*. New York, NY: HarperCollins; 2013.

Mosbergen D. Alzheimer's Researchers Probe New Treatment Paths. *Wall Street Journal*, May 22, 2022.

MSKTC. Available online at https://msktc.org/tbi/factsheets/memory-and-traumatic-brain-injury . Accessed on December 2, 2023.

Mukherjee S. *The Gene: An Intimate History*. New York, NY: Scribner; 2016.

Nahm M. 2009. Terminal Lucidity in People with Mental Illness and Other Mental Disability: An Overview and Implications for Possible Explanatory Models. *Journal of Near-Death Studies*, 28(2) Winter.

Nahm M. and Greyson B. 2009. Terminal Lucidity in Patients With Chronic Schizophrenia and Dementia: A Survey of the Literature. *Journal of Nervous and Mental Disease*, December - Volume 197 - Issue 12 - pp.942-4.

Nahm M., Greyson B., Kelley E. M., and Erlendur H. 2012. Terminal lucidity: A review and a case collection. *Archives of Gerontology and Geriatrics*, v.55, pp.138-42.

Nahm M. and Greyson B. 2013. The Death of Anna Katharina Ehmer: A Case Study in Terminal Lucidity. *OMEGA*, Vol. 68(1), 77-87.

Nestler E. J. Hidden Switches in the Mind. *Scientific American*, December 2011.

Nestler E. J. The Mind's Hidden Switches (podcast transcript) at www.scientificamerican.com/podcast/episode.cfm?id=the-minds-hidden-switches-11-11-22. Accessed on April 18, 2023.

Nisargadatta S. *I AM THAT*. Durham, NC: Acorn Press; 1973 (paperback printing 1999).

Olson K. R. When Sex and Gender Collide. *Scientific American*, September 2017.

Padawer R. What's So Bad About a Boy Who Wants to Wear a Dress? *New York Times Magazine*, August 8, 2012.

Pearsall P., Schwartz G. E., and Russek L. G. Organ Transplants And Cellular Memories. *Nexus Magazine*, April-May 2005. Originally published in *Journal of Near-Death Studies* under title "Changes in Heart Transplant Recipients that Parallel the Personalities of their Donors" in Spring 2002.

Phelps S. M. and Wedow R. What Genetics Is Teaching Us About Sexuality. *New York Times*, August 29, 2019.

Pinker S. 1997. *How the Mind Works*. New York, NY: W. W. Norton.

Pinker S. 2002. *Blank Slate: The Modern Denial of Human Nature*. New York, NY: Viking.

Pinker S. 2011. *The Better Angels of Our Nature - Why Violence has Declined*. New York, NY: Penguin Books.

Pinker S. 2013. Science Is Not Your Enemy. *The New Republic*, August 6.

Pinker S. 2018. *Enlightenment Now: The Case For Reason, Science, Humanism, and Progress*. New York, NY: Viking.

Pittelli S. 2020. Blog available at http://unwashedgenes.blogspot.com/2020/03/more-bias-in-dna-databanks.html#comment-form (accessed on 22 August 2020). Perhaps because of the controversial nature of criticizing science, I am not sure "Steven Pittelli" is this author's actual name. I have seen other names - from obviously the same person - used.

Pittelli S. 2018. Review Essay: Robert Plomin, Blueprint: How DNA Makes Us Who We Are. Available at http://logosjournal.com/2019/review-essay-robert-plomin-blueprint-how-dna-makes-us-who-we-are-cambridge-mit-press-2018/ Accessed on April 18, 2023.

Plomin R. and von Stumm S. The new genetics of intelligence. *Nature Reviews | Genetics*. 2018:19, pp. 148-159. Available at https://www.gwern.net/docs/iq/2018-plomin.pdf . Accessed on April 18, 2023.

Radin D. *Real Magic: Ancient Wisdom, Modern Science, and a Guide to the Secret Power of the Universe*. New York, NY: Harmony Books; 2018.

Reilly R. Heart and Seoul. *Sports Illustrated*, February 20, 2006.

Ricard M., Antoine L., and Richard J. D. 2014. mind of the meditator. *Scientific American*, November 2014.

Saini A and Singh S. J. A healthy island-based traditional community, the Nicobarese, had their lives upended by the 2004 tsunami and then overrun by modern life. *Scientific American*, April 2020.

Schafer A. genetics.thetech.org/ask/ask166 . Accessed on February 8, 2015.

Scharf C. The Benevolence of Black Holes. *Scientific American*, August 2012.

Shaw J. Is Epigenetics Inherited? *Harvard Magazine*, 2017. Available online at http://www.harvardmag.com/pdf/2017/05-pdfs/0517-13.pdf. Accessed on April 18, 2023.

Sheldrake R. 2011. *Dogs That Know When Their Owners Are Coming Home: Fully Revised and Updated*. New York, NY: Broadway Books.

Sheldrake R. 2012a. *The Presence of the Past*. Rochester, VT: Park Street Press.

Sheldrake R. 2012b. *Science Set Free: 10 Paths to New Discovery*. New York, NY: Deepak Chopra Books.

Sheldrake R. and Wolpert L. (Sheldrake bet) The Genome Wager. Available online at www.sheldrake.org/reactions/the-genome-wager. Accessed on November 9, 2019.

Sludge. An Amazon reader review for the *The Gene* which was submitted on June 5, 2018 by a reader named "Earnest Sludge".

Smil V. *Harvesting the Biosphere: What We Have Taken From Nature.* Cambridge, MA: MIT Press; 2015

Smith, H. (1991). *The World's Religions.* New York, NY: HarperCollins.

Sohail M., Maier R. M., Ganna A., Bloemendal A., Martin A. R., Turchin M. C., Chiang C. WK, Hirschhorn J., Daly M. J., Patterson N., Neale B., Mathieson I., Reich D., and Sunyaev S. R. Polygenic adaptation on height is overestimated due to uncorrected uncorrected stratification in genome wide association studies. eLife. March 21, 2019. Available at https://reich.hms.harvard.edu/sites/reich.hms.harvard.edu/files/inline-files/2019_SohailMaier_eLife_Height.pdf . Accessed on April 18, 2023.

Sokol J. What Animals See in the Stars, and What They Stand to Lose. *New York Times*, July 29, 2021.

Solomon A. *Far From the Tree.* New York, NY: Scribner; 2012

Spellmeyer K. After the Future. *Tricycle.* Fall 2015.

Suzuki S. *Zen Mind, Beginner's Mind.* Boulder, CO: Shambhala Publications; 2020.

Tart C. T. *The End of Materialism.* Oakland, CA: New Harbinger Publications; 2009.

Thondup T. *Peaceful Death, Joyful Rebirth.* Boston, MA: Shambhala Publications; 2005.

Tobias M. *World War III.* Santa Fe, NM: Bear & Company, Inc; 1994.

Treffert D. A. *Islands of Genius.* London, UK: Jessica Kingsley Publishers; 2010.

Trut L. and Dugatkin L. E. How to Build a Dog. *Scientific American.* May 2017.

Tucker J. *Life Before Life - A Scientific Investigation of Children's Memories of Previous Lives.* New York, NY: St. Martin's Press; 2005.

Wade N. A Dissenting Voice as the Genome is Sifted to Fight Disease. *New York Times*, September 16, 2008.

Wallace J. W. Celebrate Christmas with your kids - they already believe in God. *Fox News*, December 21, 2021.

Watson J. D. 2003. A Conversation With James D. Watson. *Scientific American*, April.

Watson J. D. with Berry A. and Davies K. 2017. *DNA: The Story of the Genetic Revolution*. New York, NY: Albert A. Knopf.

Wigner E. The Unreasonable Effectiveness of Mathematics in the Natural Sciences. Available online at https://www.maths.ed.ac.uk/~v1ranick/papers/wigner.pdf . Accessed on April 21, 2023.

Yeshe L. *Introduction to Tantra: The Transformation of Desire*. Somerville, MA: Wisdom Publications; 2001.

Young A. I. Solving the missing heritability problem. *PLOS | Genetics*. June 24, 2019. Available at https://journals.plos.org/plosgenetics/article?id=10.1371/journal.pgen.1008222 . Accessed on April 18, 2023.

Yuste R. and Church G. M. The New Century of the Brain. *Scientific American*, March 2014.

Zimmer C. Is Most of Our DNA Garbage? *New York Times Magazine*, March 8, 2015.

www.ingramcontent.com/pod-product-compliance
Lightning Source LLC
Chambersburg PA
CBHW060523080526
44586CB00012B/585